PROPERTY MANAGEMENT WITH A POPP®

The "Keys" to Profit, Occupancy and Property
Preservation for the Novice Landlord

SHERKICA MILLER-MCINTYRE,
MBA, RMP®, MPM® CANDIDATE

PROPERTY MANAGEMENT WITH A POPP®

ISBN: 978-0-578-65041-8 (Paperback)

Front Cover design/artist/Image: Lamar Bennett
Editor: Alicia Caldwell, AMC Literary Services

Printed in the United States of America

Published By Sherkica Miller-McIntyre
Publishing Consultant

SOPHISTICATED
P R E S S

Dedication

There are so many people that have been pivotal in me being here...writing a book on Property Management! They know who they are, for I make sure I thank God for them in prayer and in action. However, in this time and space, I must give special thanks to my husband Gary and children, Codi, Mackenzie, Madison, and Masyn who support...and suffer through, the madness of a busy wife and mother who happens to love being a PM!

Table of Contents

FOREWORD

I started investing in real estate, like so many others, to build wealth. And, like so many others, I had little knowledge of how to accomplish this goal. I was unaware of the tools to help me along the way, so I did what I thought was the best thing and jumped into the various roles along my journey. I was the leasing agent (who happened to be the owner of the property). I was my marketing department, took calls, did showings, handled the entire application process, and made final decisions on all tenants. Wait...there's more! I would then be their point of contact for all repairs and maintenance issues. And, oh yes, I collected rent payments, too.

I did this for about three years, on multiple properties I owned as long-term rentals. It was exhausting, to say the least. As a busy professional working full-time recruiting talent for major corporations, it was impossible for me to keep up or even have the confidence and faith to know that investment real estate was, indeed, going to be the means to build wealth, as I'd hoped. Finding Carod Properties solved my management needs.

I needed to find a property manager to stay sane and keep my day job! I researched companies and asked for recommendations. That is when I was referred to Carod Properties, by a neighbor I trusted. I was hoping our initial meeting would go well. For, a productive meeting would hopefully translate into the confidence boost I needed to see this thing through, instead of running for the hills! As a Human Resources professional, I was good at interviewing people and knew exactly what I was looking for.

Meeting Sherkica sold me on my decision to have her firm manage my properties. She had recently purchased her property management company and was in the process of growing her firm. She addressed all my concerns and was honest with what I should expect, in the short and long term, with her firm's management. Carod Properties has not only managed my rentals but has also sold multiple homes for me, as well.

If I would have had a resource like **Property Management with a POPP®** I could have saved myself a lot of headaches, time, and money. This book clearly walks through each phase of the process to successful ownership and management of investment real estate. I feel uniquely qualified to say this, as I have experienced most scenarios you could imagine and would never imagine, owning and managing rental properties. If you are looking to simplify your property management journey, look no further. This book breaks it down into bite-sized pieces and will set you on the path to profitability. Whether you are starting out or are a long-time investor, this book will add to your bottom line.

Frank T. Mitchell
Real Estate Investor

PREFACE

I want this book to be an encouragement to the person that has dreams and goals of building wealth through buying and holding real estate. When it comes to investing in real estate, I want to help investors understand that the Property Management piece, is the key to longevity. We all could purchase an income-producing property. For most potential investors, that is the simplest part of the equation. However, the process of building profits, having long-term occupancy, and the preservation of the investment can be both the impetus and the challenge of the wealth-building process.

When the management of a property falls apart, then everything else falls apart and the goal to earn an income is unrealized. I want to assist the novice individual getting into real estate that only has idealistic thoughts about the process of becoming a true and successful real estate investor. I want to help them understand the ins and outs of property management and how to build a future with real estate holdings.

Readers' Biggest Fears...

If you are afraid that you may not succeed in the handling of your investment, this book is for you. If you are concerned that you will fail at some of your real estate goals because you are not prepared for management, this book is for you. If you feel like your dreams and goals for yourself and your family rest on your ability to build your wealth through real estate holdings, this book will show you why and how the management piece is the key element in your success.

When I contemplated building wealth through investing, I did not consider the bigger picture, nor did I have a clear understanding of what happened after I received the keys to my first investment. The foundational pieces were unclear. However, once I crossed the hurdle of purchasing that first investment, went through the process of securing my first tenant, and then repeated the process with multiple properties, I realized how crucial it is to have a sound understanding of the elements of property management. This is the essential reason for writing, Property Management with a P.O.P. P®.: The Keys to Profits, Occupancy and Property Preservation for the Novice Landlord.

What are you going to learn?

Before thoroughly understanding what the strategy of buying and holding real estate looked like, I had a goal. I wanted to build wealth for myself and my family. The only way I knew to do this, at the time, was through real estate. My parents owned their home as I grew up and taught me the importance of ownership. I grasped early the notion that a home could be "lived in" for years and landlords made money hand over fist, on rentals. What I did not learn was that collecting rent was only a portion of what it takes to truly be a landlord.

In this book, you are going to learn ways to create profit that isn't just about raising the rent, learn to build a strategy to secure long-term occupancy, and plan your property preservation to maximize the usefulness of your investment. I will also add the ins and outs of property management—the good, the bad and the really ugly for those that think managing their property is simply a "walk to the bank." The "good," is collecting rent, having a tenant with no challenges, and nominal maintenance issues. The "bad," could be considered a "hiccup" every now and then, that causes you to shake your head...more than once. The "ugly," could be anything from having nonpaying tenants that dodge your every call, high turnover due to not fully understanding the market in which your investment lies, having dirty diapers left in your refrigerator to having cement poured down your drains upon move out. And, YES, that ALL happens!

Then, there is this "unknown" side of property management. This would be the side that no one can predict or predetermine the outcome. As in the case with the COVID-19 pandemic. Matters of natural disasters also fall into this realm as these are not circumstances that any of us can predict or control. However, we can be prepared in general for a crisis. If you are not well-informed about the ugly side and only see the cash flow rainbow, then you are not doing your due diligence. Not mitigating the possibility of the unknown and educating yourself, you are setting yourself up for unnecessary, avoidable frustration and failure. I am not 100% convinced that all property management PROFESSIONALS even understand these elements, so the novice landlord certainly has a learning curve to overcome.

When you hear people say things like, "Oh, you're going to make great cash flow from your rental. You will make enough that you can pay your mortgage, go on vacations, and put your kids through college," please know that yes, it is possible. But... You shall learn in this book, that your vacations may be abruptly interrupted by late-night maintenance calls. You may have to dip into the college fund to repair the polybutylene pipes that have cracked throughout the walls or to make a mortgage for the property because your tenant decides paying rent is less important than taking their own vacation.

You shall learn how occupancy works and what it looks like to sustain a tenant over a desired, contracted period. You will be introduced to The 6 X 5 Rule, which is my personal theory of creating long-term occupancy. In short, creating a system to have six tenants remain in your home for five years, giving you a strategy to pay off your mortgage, build equity and create profits.

You are also going to learn how to preserve your property and the things that you can do to ensure its life span. Many people have the idea that if someone is renting their property, then that same individual is responsible for taking care of the property, holistically. It does not quite work that way. You, as the owner, must be actively engaged in every aspect of your property to preserve it for the long term. The key to property preservation lies with the owner and their processes and procedures to ensure longevity.

Managing your own property can be a long, winding road. There is a process that you are going to be working through with every situation that arises. There is some work to be done, and no, it is not always easy. By the time you finish reading this book, you will fully understand the ins and outs of property management and say to yourself one of two things: "I'm all in and I can stomach this." Or "I'm not all in and I need to hire a professional." Please make a note. Not moving forward with your goal of owning and managing your property is not one of the options!

HOW DID I GET INTOTHIS MESS?

A "Panty Run" turned me into a Landlord

In the summer of 2005, I vividly recall sitting in a mandatory real estate class with a room full of my colleagues. Our instructor began with a small section on property management and asked the class, "How many of you are currently a landlord or operating in property management?" I proudly raised my hand, as I was a new Broker and excited about my journey. To my surprise, I was the only one in the entire class that was actively working with landlords and tenants. I still remember two comments made by the Brokers sitting nearby and the one that struck a chord the most, was, "I wonder why she would want to deal with that mess?"

At that moment, I found myself considering exactly how I had landed in property management and trying to figure out what my colleague meant by "mess."

Coincidence to some, but Divine positioning to me. But it was truly a "panty run" that changed the course of my life. While on my lunch break from my first business venture, I stopped at the mall for one of Victoria Secret's annual sales. Walking out of the store with my arms filled with pink bags, I noticed a flyer on a nearby kiosk. "Are you ready to invest in Real Estate?" asked a smiling, vaguely familiar woman on the flyer.

"Yes, I am," I thought to myself, as I quickly read the sign and continued toward the exit. When I reached the doors, it hit me that I knew the instructor hosting the advertised event! Mrs. Amy Phillips-Davis had been one of my supervisors when I was an operations analyst for a major financial institution. She was one of the most intelligent, classiest women I had ever met. She was also the only other woman I knew with a hyphenated name like mine, so the connection was immediate. I returned to the flier to gather the details about the event.

After attending her workshop, Mrs. Phillips-Davis became my family's real estate broker as well as my mentor. She helped me understand the benefits and opportunities ownership in real estate affords. Most importantly, Mrs. Phillips-Davis helped me uncover my passion for helping others learn and take intentional actions to achieve their own real estate goals.

It was by Mrs. Phillips-Davis 'encouragement that I also pursued my career in real estate and subsequently became the Broker-In-Charge and owner of Carod Properties. Carod Properties is a boutique firm located in Charlotte, NC, where I have been afforded the opportunity to not only list and sell real estate but personally manage nearly 500 properties and 1500 residents, over a 16-year period. I do not think there is a situation in property management that I have not faced personally or been made aware of in my professional circles. My accidental immersion into property management has been the catalyst to me helping 100s of investors and why it is so important to me to help even more succeed as they buy and hold investments.

I will share stories and experiences to help you learn what to expect, going far beyond sharing a few checklists or a procedural manual. I want you to experience what I have experienced over 16 years of being a professional property manager and managing my own family's portfolio.

In short, I have been blessed to learn from mentors, colleagues, and on-the-job. Now, I feel it is my duty to share much of what I've learned so that by the end of this book, I can call you, my colleague!

How Did You Get into This "MESS"?

Are you an Accidental Landlord?

An Accidental Landlord is someone who has been forced into using a property that they own, as an investment property. A few ways this may become a reality, are:

- Inheritance of a property that, for whatever reason, you are either not able to or not wishing to live in

- Being unable to sell your property

- Two households (and, two separate homeowners) becoming one

While you may never have intended to become a landlord, it may be the best option for you and the "unwanted" property. Even those who are considered experts in the real estate game have properties they intended to flip or sell, right away, and either the market or other circumstances prevented it. The difference between them and the reluctant, accidental landlord is perspective. Winston Churchill said, "A pessimist sees the difficulty in every opportunity; an optimist sees the opportunity in every difficulty." Often, that is what separates success from missed opportunity, the ability to regroup and make the best of the situation.

My husband and I are great examples of accidental landlords. When we decided that we were going to begin our real estate investment journey, the goal was to purchase brand new homes at a discount from builders, lease the houses to "almost" qualified tenants, and resell the property within 12-18 months. This process is commonly known as a lease option, and it worked well for us until the market took an unexpected turn between 2009-2010.

We were forced to hold on to properties due to the fact, the "almost qualified" tenants could no longer get qualified and home values took a dive. The positive aspect is that we had properties that were new, our maintenance was low and the residents we placed in the homes truly loved the property. To this day, we still own several of these homes, but we neither intended to be landlords nor had we educated ourselves on how to profit beyond the planned, eventual sell.

We did not have the policies and procedures in place to handle long-term maintenance and occupancy issues. The learning curve was significant. Looking back, I can say that had I opened a book such as this, to provide me a realistic view of what was involved in holding rentals, I could have saved myself a few major headaches. The positive aspect is that I learned enough in those early years to discover that being a landlord and managing for others would be an ideal career path.

If you are reading this book, it is likely that you are planning your initial steps into the "mess" better known as property management with a clearer vision than myself. Whether managing a single property or small portfolio for yourself or in the early stages of managing for others, it is ideal that you take the time to prepare. I am thrilled to be a part of your journey, so let's dive right in!

KEYS TO MAKING A PROFIT WITH YOUR RENTAL PROPERTY

CHAPTER I

CRUNCHING NUMBERS

As a real estate investor, (that's you, even if you became one by default), you have to think bigger and more detailed than the "rent collected is cash flow" thought process. Constantly be mindful and duty-bound to account for the fluctuation in non-monthly but regular costs/expenses like vacancy, repairs, and capital expenditures (replacements items like roofing, appliances, plumbing, etc.). Keeping these things in mind, along with regular monthly expenses, is a vital way to maintain consistent cash flow and opportunities to build.

Knowledge Is Powerful!

Your real estate portfolio hinges on one simple aspect: the numbers. These numbers are the foundation of any real estate investment. They provide transparency and can help you make the decisions that will get you closer to your investment goals and certainly essential to building your wealth through real estate holdings. Each of your investments should be initially evaluated and broken down using the below methods to help you determine the performance of a potential investment or to understand your current property. This helps weigh your options when either selecting a new property or evaluating your current property.

Return on Investment (ROI)

How do you know if you are getting a good return on your real estate investment? Effectively calculating the return on investment (ROI) of your income property is critical to know how your investment is performing, or when comparing one investment to another. Whether that other one is in your portfolio, one you're considering acquiring, or the competition. To successfully decide whether a property is worth buying, an investor must run the numbers to calculate two types of returns: Cash-on-Cash Return on Investment, and Total Return on Investment.

Cash on Cash Return on Investment

The Cash-on-Cash (COC) ROI is the before-tax cash flow (BTCF) divided by your initial cash investment. The formula looks like this:

Cash on Cash Return on Investment = BTCF / Initial Cash Investment.

Your before-tax cash flow is calculated by subtracting your annual mortgage payment from your Net Operating Income (NOI). The net operating income is simply the property's total income minus its total operating expenses. (Note that mortgage payments are not part of operating expenses.)

Total Return on Investment

The total return on investment (TROI) provides a better and more complete measure of a property's financial performance. That is because it factors in amortization and appreciation gained over time.

Total ROI = (BTCF + Net Sales Proceeds – Initial Cash Investment) / Initial Cash Investment. To calculate the TROI, one must project the BTCF for each year of expected ownership as well as the net sales proceeds from the sale of the property.

Amortization

Low Pay-Down. As you collect rent, you take care of your mortgage and maybe even retain some funds. Over time, the property will be paid for by the tenant paying your mortgage, building wealth automatically. To make this concept clearer, pretend for a moment you owned a property that you bought for $1,000,000 with a mortgage for $800,000, and it made $0 in cash flow (it "broke even") and never climbed in value. However, after that thirty-year mortgage is paid off, you'll now have a property worth $1,000,000 for which you never actually had to save. Your tenant paid it off due to the "loan pay-down."

Market Growth and Buying at the Right Time Appreciation." Appreciation" is when the value of your property increases. Historically, in America, property value increases annually, on average, 3%. While this is not guaranteed and therefore not reliable, there is another form of appreciation that can assure your property's value will increase, and therefore should be a part of your investment strategy. "Forced Appreciation" is the concept of increasing the value by physically improving the property. In other words, the increase of your property's value—and in turn bettering your investment...BUILDING—is wholly in your hands. Listen to the experts, make smart financial decisions and the BUILDING will take care of itself.

Capitalization Rate

The Capitalization Rate (also known as "Cap Rate") is used to compare an income property with other similar income properties. It can also be used to place a value on a property based on the income it generates. The Cap Rate is calculated by taking the property's net operating income (NOI) and dividing it by the property's fair market value (FMV). The higher the Cap Rate, the better the property's income and market value. The Cap Rate is calculated as follows:

Capitalization Rate = Net Operating Income / Market Value

The Cap Rate merely represents the projected return for one year, as if the property was bought without financing ("all cash"). However, since we do not normally buy property using all cash, we would use other measures such as the cash-on-cash return, to evaluate a property's financial performance.

Rent-to-Value Ratio

The Rent-to-Value (R/V) Ratio provides a quick measure of a property's cash flow and income potential. It is conceptually similar to the Price-to-Earnings ratio used to determine whether common stocks are over- or under-valued. My professional opinion is that an R/V ratio of 0.7% is a minimum, with an ideal number closer to 1.0%. Obviously, the higher the better!

The R/V ratio is calculated by dividing the gross monthly rental income into the current fair market value of the property. For example, a property that is worth $100,000 today and rents for $1,000 per month would have an R/V ratio of 1.0%.

I use the R/V ratio to quickly evaluate every single property we look at before we consider doing further due diligence on it. It is one of my many "rules of thumb" to quickly screen for potentially good properties.

I know you felt as if you were back in your high school finance or economics class after this chapter but trust me these calculations and formulas will be of great use to you, especially if your goal is to build a successful and diverse portfolio of properties in the future. Being able to evaluate your rental property from a strictly numbers perspective is essential. In property management the "**numbers**" will help you refrain from becoming emotionally involved, which happens from time to time.

CHAPTER II

SHOW ME THE MONEY!

The fluctuating real estate market can have many people thinking of what is best for them and what's next? Many markets, unfortunately, even have some postponing the American dream of personal home ownership, while others have been able to capitalize on record lows in mortgage interest rates. Simply said, in some areas, it is the perfect time to become a landlord. So, what exactly does that mean and what steps should you be taking to join in on the "fun"? This thought process is where being an intentional landlord derives.

If I have said it once, I have said it 1,000 times, "Do your research." Just because mortgage rates are low, you should not take that as an invitation to buy the very first property that appeals to you. There is much more involved with being a landlord: listings, finding tenants, contracts, property maintenance, multiple budgets to manage (yours and your rental). The list goes on and on. Instead of listing all the things you probably were not considering, I am just going to give you a few steps to take to set you up for income property success!

After the initial decision to invest in an income property, there's usually much more work to do. I aim to prepare and inform you, not to discourage you. Being a profitable landlord is possible, but it is certainly a process. Many individuals amass their wealth through real estate. There is absolutely no reason you cannot be one of them if you have a solid foundation and plan.

Landlords who are engaged in the process are the most successful, now that does not mean 100% hands-on but it does mean you are active in your portfolio's success and not far removed even if you decide to allow someone else to manage it for you. The individuals that are more engaged understand that their property is their most valuable asset and one of the most expensive things they will own outside of their primary residence. Some landlords believe they only need to do limited things while "managing" their property. However, that's not necessarily true. There are a lot of things that a landlord can do to create long-term occupancy, extend the life of their property, and increase its value while making the investment profitable and marketable to potential occupants. Let's dive into your best next steps in putting your intent into action!

I knew I wanted to build a fortune in real estate right after we purchased our first home. With the help of my mentor (post-license), my husband and I purchased our first investment property that honestly was twice the size of our own home, as was the mortgage. I was so excited that those two factors never popped into my head until after we closed. Had I thought too hard about it, I would have never taken the leap. As stated earlier, our initial strategy was to buy, do lease options for "nearly" qualified buyers, and sell to the resident within 12-18 months. We would strategically price the home for at least a 20-30K profit along with obtaining the monthly cash flow.

The strategy was perfect as we would only purchase brand new homes and thus the maintenance would be nominal, with no turnover process and the likelihood the tenant would be late or miss payments would be low based on their desire to purchase in the short term.

The goal was to complete this process at least 15-20 times to build capital for future projects, pay off our home and invest in other ventures. We were very clear on our WHY and the process of "How" wasn't too bad. EXCEPT...! The market changed within the next few years and the lease options became long-term rentals.

However, after our first few transactions, I realized, "Wow, it's really not that difficult to find a good tenant. And, just maybe buying and holding was a better long-term option or at least enough to weather the market crash."

We learned how to advertise for the rentals, make the houses look desirable, and price them well. By doing so...the tenants would come and stay. Prayerfully!

So, I started to evaluate the numbers, i.e., the income we were making earning $200, $300, $400 in rent. It made inescapable, financial sense to keep repeating the process.

Soon, I could see that we only needed a few more properties to be able to continue towards our goals. Going through the process the first time made it easier for me to say, "Yeah, I think we can do it again." In my opinion, it's like having children. Once you have two, then the 3rd, 4th...the rest, come easier. Then, you can have 20 and can really say, "I got this!"

So, ask yourself, why do YOU want to become a landlord? What do you want to accomplish with a rental property? I will say, it's fine if you don't have an answer, just yet.

Some of the most common answers are:

- **Monthly Residual**—Are you looking for the monthly residual income that comes from the rental income (minus any expenses)? Is your goal monthly cash flow? Many investors would identify Cash Flow as their primary reason for pursuing investment property and becoming a landlord.

- **Long-Term Wealth Building**—If there is still a mortgage, the rent collected can pay some, if not all, of the mortgage. This is most beneficial if you carry the property as a rental until it is paid for, making the rent garnered, thereafter, 100% profit.

- **Building Equity**—The market may change, making the property worth more when you opt to sell, later. Again, if this is the case, the mortgage will have been paid down, making more of the selling price go into your pocket rather than paying off the mortgage.

- **TAX BREAKS/INCENTIVES**—Interest, Depreciation, Repairs, Local/Long Distance Travel Expenses, Home Office Expenses, Being your own boss. You may just like being a landlord and have stumbled onto a business rather than an inconvenience.

The opportunities abound if you are willing to do the work involved. Work can be anything from physical labor (renovations and/or ongoing maintenance) to researching the legalities involved. Again, without risk, there can be no reward. The reward possibly can be great, if you take the risk and follow through with hard work. Just be clear on your why and stay focused on the strategies that help you achieve your goals.

Understanding the Local Market

Whether or not you are purchasing your investment or converting your own home into a rental, you need to understand the market in which your property is located. Understanding the current market and what may possibly happen to the local market over the next few years, is key to your ability to make a profit, have long-term occupancy, and even the cost of property preservation.

Often, we look at the news and see stories, facts, and figures on a national rather than local level. This means that your perspective of your investment can be based on information outside of the market in which you will do business. This can cause major issues, as you must gain a reasonable understanding of your local market to make judgments and forecasts on what the real estate market will do, over the next one to five years.

Here are the key factors in helping you understand the local market where you will be managing one or several rental units:

Who's Renting

Understanding the demographics of the city in which you are located is key. This vital knowledge helps determine, down to a community level, the likelihood of your ability to lease at a certain price point and the potential for long-term tenancy. Is your rental property located in a high, mid, or low-income range community; is the property in a developing or challenging area, or do you have a specialty home (such as in a senior community), that may limit your potential resident pool; or are you in the heart of a college town. This is important for you to know how to best structure your rental.

Affordability

Ultimately, though you want to have rent as profitable as possible, your local real estate market is going to be dependent on the people's ability to afford the homes.

Two key components to affordability are the household income and the rental price. Placing these two factors together can help you price your property for the long term. Understand that if the household income median can't afford the rent you're seeking, you may need to adjust your pricing strategy.

When you put all these factors together, you can much better understand your local real estate market. Only then, can you effectively devise how to best price your property for successful, continuous rental.

Employment

Employment plays a tremendous role in the local real estate markets. It is how people afford to rent your home. Most experts would state that people live near their jobs or the access to employment, such as public transportation or commuting stations. Therefore, your property's proximity to employment opportunities is essential.

Do the research to gain access to your local employment rates. Many of these figures can be gained through a simple online search. Understanding your local area's employment rates can help you determine the current local market trends and what they will do in the next few years. Continuous employment and employment opportunities are essential to retaining paying tenants.

Supply

Supply is the total of houses for rent or units available on the market, at a given time in your area. The typical benchmark for this is 4-6 months, which is what you as a buy and hold investor should consider whether you are starting, maintaining, or growing your portfolio. If there is less than a 6 months' supply of houses, there is a potential for a shortage. A shortage could raise demand and potentially raise prices. Good for landlords. Not so good for tenants.

If there is more than 4-6 months 'supply of rental houses, then there could potentially be a surplus, which could cause problems or even slight price drops. The 2009-2013 years are examples of this where landlords had to dramatically drop their rental rates to keep up with the competition and surplus of houses.

Understanding the Optimum Rent Price Point/ Set Your Rental Price to Property Value (Not Market Trends)

For me, maximizing the market means that you look at the market at the time and determine your rent based on market value, not just out of thin air. Taking the time to evaluate market rents to price your property accurately, is crucial.

The goal is to price your rental at a price point that will get it rented quickly. You do not want a rental property to sit on the market, empty for a long period of time, because you will be losing money. If the property has debt service or a mortgage, you could lose more money waiting for a tenant than you would by lowering the rent, even by a nominal amount. Once a property is rented, you will be positioned to grow the rental amount.

When I am having conversations with property owners on how to price their property, many may say to me "Sherkica, I want to price my property at $1,800." When I ask, "Well, how did you arrive at that number?" I will often hear, "Oh, I just want to make $300 a month on that property."

I must stop them and use this moment as an opportunity to educate. I advise, "Well, that's really not how it works. We need to do a full comparative analysis of all the rentals in your area that are similar to your property and determine what that looks like. Because, when you put your house on the market, those are the properties you will be competing against."

If your rental is priced above market rents, even if you find a tenant, what is the likelihood that the tenant is going to remain in the property for five years? If you price your rental well at the beginning based on the market, then it allows you to have growth. It allows you to retain the tenant longer. In turn, that lessens your turnkey expenses and hopefully increases your profits.

I manage a property that is near uptown Charlotte. It has been completely renovated. It is a beautiful unit, but I believed the client was about $200 to $300 over what the market dictated as a competitive rent. In the clients 'minds, all they were considering was the location, a property near uptown Charlotte, a highly desirable area. What they did not consider, was that they had completed a beautiful renovation, on an older home in an older community, that had not yet been enveloped into the re-gentrification process. One day the property will warrant a higher rental price, but at my intake, we were not yet quite there.

I always calculate the loss of income. If you put a house on the market that is overpriced and it stays empty for one to two months, you might as well have lowered the rents on the property, because those dollars are lost to the waiting game. It just does not make good financial sense to price it high. These clients waited almost three months to get their property rented. They finally did get it rented, on a short-term lease, because the tenant wanted to be in the area for work. The client should have taken my advice and priced the unit at the current market value earlier.

The leased tenant only desired to do a 6-month lease which ultimately will require the landlord to have earlier make-ready costs and remarketing fees. An earlier, correct pricing strategy, versus a whimsical desired price, would have saved time and money. At the time of the writing of this book, the property did have a one-year lease...at my initial recommended rental rate. I promise, I never once uttered, "I told you so!"

The rental market tends to fluctuate, which is why most experts do not recommend following trends. Instead, you should establish the rental rate based on your property value. In general, a rate between .8 and 1.1% of the home's value is the average. This may not align with your vision of making $1000.00 a month cash flow but it allows you to be strategic. Some variation is expected, of course. Checking comparable offerings in the area can help you settle on the appropriate price, for successfully securing a tenant, in a good or down market.

Becoming a property investor can be challenging, but it can also be rewarding and lucrative. By taking these steps, you will start off on the right path toward creating passive income. You may even find that being a landlord earns you enough to continue investing in even more property.

In addition to comparing market rents or pricing, a successful investor compares property conditions.

Comparing conditions helps you determine rent pricing and helps assess your expenses in preparing the property for rent. You always want to consider your mortgage, your insurance, management fees, and a threshold for expenses as part of your pricing strategy. The goal is to have a holistic view of what your price should be, your expenses on the property, its overall condition, and what things you can do to retain a tenant over time.

CHAPTER III

TAX BENEFITS

The final wealth generator and "number" to know, regarding real estate, are the tax benefits associated with owning property. The U.S. government favors real estate investors and uses the tax system to encourage the purchase and leasing of properties. From extra tax write-offs to the lack of "self-employment tax," to the 1031-exchange and more. Real estate investors can pay significantly less tax than other business owners. Then, the most diligent and focused investors will use the extra cash to buy more properties or pay off the loan faster, helping to build greater wealth.

Here are the key tax benefits:

- Depreciation
- Interest
- Ability to Write Off Expenses

Keeping Good Records

When you make the transition from owner to an investor, and yes there is a difference, there are many things that can cause stress to the novice investor. In situations where you are lacking knowledge, I cannot stress vehemently enough, ask an expert. The consequences and penalties can be too high...and expensive, by assuming or relying on inaccurate or outdated information.

One such area is record keeping. New investors often find themselves in a quandary over what to keep and what to throw away. Neither the "keep everything" nor the "probably don't need it" attitude is very effective or recommended when it comes to matters of business. For general-purpose records retention, there are a few "best practices" that can be used as guidelines on what to keep or throw away and essentially help you to develop personal criteria for record-keeping:

1. **Some items should NEVER be thrown away.** If an item/document cannot be duplicated or reproduced, a good rule of thumb is to establish a system for "permanent records" filing. You should take further precautions, such as backing up copies in the cloud, and/or securing them in a protected safe or lockbox. Examples: Income tax returns; legal documents; vital records (birth/marriage certificates), trusts, and audits.

2. **Business records should be considered as "permanent records."** Businesses (LLS's, S-Corps) are held to a much more stringent standard than an individual. To add insult to injury, many individual industries have their own set of standards, making some things/documents more important in one industry, whereas it may be insignificant in another. ASK AN EXPERT. Then...LISTEN TO THE ANSWER(S)!

3. **Keep tax records for 6 years.** The IRS may go back as far as 6 years for errors and/or incorrect claims and deductions. Therefore, you must place the utmost importance on thorough, tax-related record/document keeping. This includes:
   a. Bank, personnel and payroll, vendor invoices, accident claims, and records on purchases and sales, to name a few.

4. **Keep everyday paperwork for 3 years.** Probably no one wants to know how much your electric bill was on a given date, but some non-essential, non-tax-related documents may warrant retaining, for as much as 3 years:
   a. Monthly financials, credit card statements, utility records, and medical bills.

5. **ORGANIZATION is KEY!** When developing your personal system for record-keeping for your

investment a system to stay organized should be the cornerstone of whatever method you choose. Day to day, week to week a myriad of documents will potentially cross your desk. The only way to make heads or tails of this influx of paperwork is to first establish a well-thought, all-inclusive system before even the first document hits your desk.

You will find, once you have your system in place, that knowledge of all these best practices is invaluable. When your hobby, passion, accidental venture becomes a business which is often the case with novice landlords, everything, especially your thinking, will need to shift. Success will depend on how effectively EVERY area of your business is handled. And the area of proper and efficient record keeping lends itself to almost every other aspect of your business. Take the time to do it right or suffer the consequences, instead of reaping the rewards.

So, make sure that your records are thorough with regards to:

- Advertising

- Cleaning and maintenance

- Commissions paid to rental agents

- Homeowner association/condo dues

- Insurance premiums

- Legal fees

- Mortgage interest

- Taxes

- Utilities

There may be and most likely are items missing from the above list that are specific to you and your real estate investment business. That is why, and this has been advised many times before, that you secure and maintain a relationship with a professional whose business acumen is business tax filing. You wouldn't let just anyone that can hold a pair of scissors loose on your head of hair, would you? NO!

You employ the services of a professional, educated for that purpose, whose business it is to provide desired results in their field. With a haircut, you only get a bad head of hair for a while. With taxes, there is a unique set of unpalatable problems that go along with choosing the wrong path. While the U.S. government favors real estate investors, one can quickly fall out of favor. One easy way to do so is not to have proper records to support your business. Handle your investment accordingly and reap all the benefits that Uncle Sam has to offer you.

CHAPTER IV

CASH FLOW IS NOT LIMITED TO RENT

As you set up and grow your portfolio, you will find that adding valuable services, that provide ease and additional comfort for yourself and tenants, can create major profit centers. Fees assessed for not aligning with your preferred processes and procedures can also create profit opportunities.

Examples of these fees include in-person or online application processing fees based on your preference, convenience fees for payment processing, monthly credit reporting fees, pet fees (not deposits), maintenance calls that are tenant responsibilities, and access to amenities if not offered through the rental amount but available to the resident such as community gym and pool access.

Ensure that any fee you assess the tenant has been reviewed by your attorney for accuracy and within compliance with all local or state laws. The goal is not to "nickel and dime" your tenant. However, valid charges for business operations and tenant administration should be a part of your business plan. Not doing so leaves money on the table that is completely within reason to collect.

A few examples of fees that you may charge a tenant within your municipality is application fees and other administrative fees such as additional copies of leases and addendum, completing documentation for third parties on the tenant's behalf, or payment processing fees that are made known at the time of the lease or those in exception to your normal processes and procedures.

As a landlord, I have created a stream of income-based specifically on administrative fees that are then used for savings for any future vacancy or maintenance. These fees have equated to $500-$1500 a year per property.

Additional fees that may be applicable to your tenant will be discussed later in the book.

CHAPTER V

TAKE THE PROFIT PLEDGE

Repeat after me, "I shall continuously CONTROL AND MITIGATE overall expenses to the best of my ability!"

No matter how one finds themselves immersed in the world of being a landlord, the key is to understand the numbers and how to control as much of those numbers as possible.

Because let's face it, it's not just all about collecting rent and making cash flow magically. There is a true science to both the longevity and sustainability of your investment. So, if you are really about your business, you anticipate expenses and repairs and have incorporated a maintenance routine that will hopefully mitigate the need for untimely repairs. But no matter how diligent you are, there are always going to be repairs that come up based on normal wear and tear and hopefully only a few from accidental tenant damage or malice intent.

To add to that, if you are in the industry long enough, there are going to be repair-needy tenants. These will be tenants who seem to have an issue with their residence every other day. Things happen and a tenant should never be dissuaded from giving notice of a need for repair. However, the "repair-needy" tenant would be one that makes frivolous, time-consuming requests like, their tap water is not cold enough when it's 1000 degrees outside or the AC is not keeping the house at their preferred 65 degrees...WHEN IT'S 1000 DEGREES OUTSIDE!

It is vital that you maintain control of your expenses and carrying costs if your property investment is to remain at all profitable. The key to doing that is minimizing unnecessary expenses. That can be done in several ways when it comes to repairs, but a surefire way (and this will sound very familiar) is to address repairs in a very clear, detailed way in the **language of your lease**. To do that:

- Give a clear indication of what is outside of your responsibility, like wear and tear.

- Advise of, and stick to, a clear maintenance schedule. A tenant may be less likely to complain about an issue that they know will soon be addressed during a regular maintenance schedule. However, advise that it is also their responsibility to make you aware of anything that becomes a more **urgent** issue.

- Advise of a kind of deductible for repair calls (especially, repeated) that result in no need for repair. In other words, "My AC isn't keeping my home cool." (And it's 1000 degrees outside.) If you have your maintenance staff, come out, or worse a specialist, and nothing is found to be wrong or the problem is tenant error, the costs associated with the call will be theirs.

Note that in the scenario above, educating your tenant on how the HVAC system works may be a good way to lessen maintenance calls during the hot summer months. I have learned quite a bit about the mechanics of a home and learning to communicate that knowledge with residents has helped them understand the functionality and the operations of their home lessening maintenance costs.

Again, you never want to give an indication that a tenant's concerns are not of the utmost concern to you. You do, however, need to make it clear that their calls, necessary and unnecessary, incur a cost to you. To maintain the profitability of your property/investment/business and not have to pass on your rising costs to your tenants, you absolutely must keep these things in check. Knowledge is power! When you know what you must do to be successful, own it, and make decisions accordingly.

KEYS TO OCCUPANCY: WHO, HOW, HOW LONG AND WHY IS A RESIDENT OCCUPYING YOUR PROPERTY?

CHAPTER VI

MAINTAINING OCCUPANCY

I have advised you what steps to take when considering a rental-purchase and how to evaluate the market to make a profit. This section will discuss how to secure and maintain occupancy and avoid the cycle of temporary tenants and long-term vacancies.

One way to avoid paying for your rental when you have no tenant is to have a solid leasing/rental agreement. Having a solid, legally vetted contract with no loopholes or ambiguities will protect you financially. As much as the internet provides resources, I highly suggest you have an attorney draft your lease based on your state laws and in compliance with all federal laws.

The lease is your blueprint, for the tenant and you to follow, which should clearly spell out the terms, expectations, responsibilities, and ramifications for violations. The lease is the most important document you as a landlord will have and it can be designed specifically for your property if it complies with the law. A strong lease will keep you from going to "landlord" jail and ensure your tenant is held responsible for its provisions.

For example, if your tenant leaves the property prior to the end of their lease, a proper contract will make them financially responsible for the duration of their signed lease term. This may not get you a new renter immediately, however, you can recoup your outstanding rent while you search for another tenant.

Here are a few other things you can do and/or implement to try to maintain long-term occupancy that can be incorporated into the lease.

Amenities, Amenities, Amenities. Having an attractive property makes the grass less green on the other side. Be judicious in how you spend to upgrade but make your property as attractive as possible to prospective tenants and to keep them. They won't need to upgrade if they are already living somewhere with all the bells and whistles.

Inclusions. If your property is energy-efficient, it is a good idea to include some or all utilities. Property owners are moving away from this because of the potential for abuse. However, with the proper contract, holding the tenant responsible for expenses outside specified/average use, you can safeguard yourself from abuse.

Ease of Access. Your tenants 'lives are just as busy as yours. One way to make your property an appealing place to live is by making yourself available or easily accessible. An email and 800# allow for a feeling of immediacy and 24-hour access. You might also consider providing a means to pay online. Being able to forego checks, money orders, and stamps as well as provide a way to avoid late payments, is very attractive and not something everyone provides. More and more, people are paying all their bills, when possible, online. This amenity also provides an air of professionalism.

Research. I know I am starting to sound like a broken record. However, I would not keep saying it if it wasn't so darn on point! Knowing the comparable properties and pricing in your area is not just something you do during the property search. You also need to keep up with this information after your purchase of a rental. Know what other properties are requesting for rent, popular upgrades, and concessions provided for multi-year leases. The list goes on and on.

Familiarize yourself with the market, see where you exceed market demands (as you might even be able to get more rent), or see where you are lacking so that you may address areas of concern and stay competitive.

The '6 X 5' Rule™ (Create your own rules)

Being a landlord is so much more than owning multiple properties and collecting cash flow smoothly. It can be rewarding and very lucrative when done with proper planning and due diligence in all aspects of the process. Maintaining occupancy is arguably one of the most important tasks involved with owning an income property. After all, it's not really an income property if it's not generating income! Hmmm, something to think about.

As discussed in several areas of the book, two key elements of being successful in holding investments are controlling expenses and consistent occupancy. I created a rule to assist my clients to strategically plan for longevity. The '6 X 5 'Rule™ is designed to plan for 6 tenants to occupy your property for 5 years each. No one can guarantee occupancy however a few strategies can aid in maintaining a long-term tenant.

The screening process, if too stringent, can limit prospects and be an indicator that more mobile residents will be attracted, those only residing for 1-2 years versus 5-6.

Instead of having a policy that includes an automatic lease increase at renewals, it may be best to evaluate each tenant's lease renewal based on their performance as much as it is based on your overall expenses and the market. This will give you the opportunity to negotiate a lease renewal for another year without scaring the tenant and prompting them to look at other options.

Learn what features of your home attracted your tenant to apply and secure. Enhance these features as you are able and keep these well maintained such as fences, pools, fireplaces, and fire pits.

Ask questions of your residents to find out what you can do to help retain them for additional time. In some cases, you may not be able to meet their requests. However, if even a small reduction of rent is requested for an interim, it may be well worth it to avoid the make-ready costs and vacancy costs.

Be open to subsidized housing recipients and do the research with the local agencies to determine if residency averages show 5 years.

The goal of The 6 x 5 Rule™ is to do all that is within your power to have a long-term, good-paying tenant that loves your home. In so doing, their experience with you, feelings about the home will translate into longevity. That longevity will then create an avenue for paying off your home based on a 15- or 30-year amortization schedule.

Processes and Procedures of Managing

If you have never read any resource previously before opening this book, you will learn how important this portion of the book is to your investment journey. Fair Housing is the most important information you will need to know—up-down, inside, and out, and around and around—during your journey as a landlord.

This vital information is key to how you market your home, create the qualifications for your applications, make final decisions on housing, and how to avoid making amateur mistakes in your general interaction with potential tenants and eventual residents.

In fact, I wanted to ensure you had the info firsthand and decided to share the proceeding, directly from HUD. Read it, copy, paste and print it. Post it in your office! Yes, it is that important.

Fair Housing

The Fair Housing Act of 1968 is also known as Title VIII of the Civil Rights Act of 1968. The Act explicitly defines a list of prohibited practices involving housing, including sales, rentals, advertising, and financing. Its primary prohibitions make it unlawful to refuse to sell, rent to, or negotiate with any person because of that person's race, color, religion, sex, familial status, handicap, or national origin. The Fair Housing Amendments Act of 1988 added extensive provisions to apply to discrimination against disabled persons and families with children 18 years of age or under. Municipalities, local government units, cities, and federal agencies are subject to the law.

Basic Facts About Fair Housing

What Housing is Covered?
The Fair Housing Act covers most housing. In some circumstances, the Act exempts owner-occupied buildings with no more than four units, single-family housing sold or rented without the use of a broker, and housing operated by organizations and private clubs that limit occupancy to members.

What Is Prohibited?

In the Sale and Rental of Housing: No one may take any of the following actions based on race, color, national origin, religion, sex, familial status, or handicap (disability):

- Refuse to rent or sell housing
- Refuse to negotiate for housing
- Make housing unavailable
- Deny a dwelling
- Set different terms, conditions, or privileges for sale or rental of a dwelling
- Provide different housing services or facilities
- Falsely deny that housing is available for inspection, sale, or rental
- For profit, persuade owners to sell or rent (blockbusting) or
- Deny anyone access to or membership in a facility or service (such as a multiple listing service) related to the sale or rental of housing.

In Mortgage Lending: No one may take any of the following actions based on race, color, national origin, religion, sex, familial status, or handicap (disability):

- Refuse to make a mortgage loan
- Refuse to provide information regarding loans
- Impose different terms or conditions on a loan, such as different interest rates, points, or fees
- Discriminate in appraising property
- Refuse to purchase a loan or

- Set different terms or conditions for purchasing a loan.

In Addition: It is illegal for anyone to:
- Threaten, coerce, intimidate, or interfere with anyone exercising a fair housing right or assisting others who exercise that right
- Advertise or make any statement that indicates a limitation or preference based on race, color, national origin, religion, sex, familial status, or handicap. This prohibition against discriminatory advertising applies to single-family and owner-occupied housing that is otherwise exempt from the Fair Housing Act.

Housing Opportunities for Families

Unless a building or community qualifies as housing for older persons, it may not discriminate based on familial status. That is, it may not discriminate against families in which one or more children under 18 live with:
- A parent,
- A person who has legal custody of the child or children or,
- The designee of the parent or legal custodian, with the parent or custodian's written permission.

Familial status protection also applies to pregnant women and anyone securing legal custody of a child under 18.

Exemption: Housing for older persons is exempt from the prohibition against familial status discrimination if:

- The HUD Secretary has determined that it is specifically designed for and occupied by elderly persons under a Federal, State, or local government program or,
- It is occupied solely by persons who are 62 or older or,
- It houses at least one person who is 55 or older in at least 80 percent of the occupied units and adheres to a policy that demonstrates an intent to house persons who are 55 or older.

Source: **HUD Fair Housing**

FRESH CORN (FRSH CRN)

Now that you have read through the information, one of the easiest ways to remember who and what is covered with Fair Housing Laws is the acronym FRESH CORN (FRSH CRN). I learned this in my very first real estate course, and it stuck in my head. The acronym lists the protected classes:

Familial Status
Race
Sex
Handicap
Color
Religion
National Origin

This is a perfect way for you to remain aware of the protected classes and to ensure you do not create a process or procedure, make any comments, or take actions that violate any of the above categories. Your goal is to make money to build wealth and the best way to protect yourself from having to spend it on bail is to adhere to Fair Housing laws!

How to Market Effectively

Based on your initial market research, you should be clear on where your property falls within the market. With this information, you can begin to strategize the best marketing plan. Most prospective tenants use the internet to locate their properties. How your property shows up is important. Thus, a proper online presence is essential to prompt placement.

When you are doing online marketing, a vital part of successfully finding tenants is how your property is presented. If you are not advertising your property online and responding to every inquiry, you might be missing out on potentially lucrative rental opportunities.

You can attract good tenants by ensuring your online reputation is worthy of them, and by using a strict application process to weed out potential problem renters. Note that the larger websites such as Zillow, Trulia, Hot Pads, and Zumper are great places to advertise, along with social media. You may also hire a real estate professional to assist you with listing your property in the local Multiple Listing Service which will feed to Realtor.com.

As a reminder, bring out the best in your property by highlighting its features and benefits. Potential residents are savvy and are doing their comparisons of pricing and overall appearance based on their online findings. Take the time to ensure your property makes the prospect want to know more and SEE the property. Enough so that they will send a quality inquiry and even follow up with a call.

Here are a few ways to capture the essence of your rental property to create interest and lessen the time on the market:

Highlighting the security of your property in multiple ways for prospective renters is an essential factor. You can protect your investment and provide peace of mind for your tenants by keeping the home secure.

Another strategy to stay under budget with features of the homes is mixing low- and mid-cost features. For example, you can plant shrubs or bushes under windows, making it difficult for intruders to access the house. Citrus trees, pyracantha, and roses can be thorny deterrents to would-be criminals. Improved lighting can also help reduce criminal activity, or at the very least, help increase renters ' confidence in their new home's security. A home security system is another feature you may consider, but the average cost totals around $675, plus regular monitoring costs through a company or service.

All the above are incentives that both attract new renters and are low cost easily absorbed within the rental price.

Promote the Sellable Features

When preparing your house for a tenant, check a few boxes. For example, tenants prioritize location over all other features so give information in your marketing that highlights the area and what a resident can access. Proximity to things such as shopping, highways and major thoroughfares, restaurants, public transportation, dog parks, and school districts. The availability of parking, laundry facilities, and decent-sized yards are also top considerations.

Of course, there are other noteworthy aspects of the property that you should include, if not highlight, in your marketing strategy. Key things, especially features that are trending on the market, are certainly advisable to include—like an open floor plan and any updates of things that could potentially affect one's enjoyment of the property.

CHAPTER VII

SUBSIDY OR NO SUBSIDY

Subsidized housing is considered government-sponsored economic assistance aimed towards alleviating housing costs and expenses for individuals with low to moderate incomes. Often, this term is referred to as "affordable housing" and synonymous, in most landlords' eyes, to Section 8 or the Housing Choice Voucher program. However, subsidies can be in the form of direct paid housing, non-profit housing, public housing, rent supplements, and some forms of co-operative and private-sector housing.

Housing vouchers allow a family to choose where they rent and pay up to 30 percent of their household income toward rent, with the voucher covering the gap. Landlords do have to agree to accept the face value of the voucher and cannot charge any additional rents outside of the voucher.

Vouchers are limited and often difficult for holders to use based on the market and unfortunately due to the perceptions of landlords. Taking time to review this chapter, can help you determine if accepting vouchers is mandatory and how it may be beneficial.

As a landlord, you should take time to understand what types of subsidies may be available in your area and if by local municipality ordinances or state law you are required to accept applications for an individual with housing vouchers. Many cities across the United States have added protections within their local ordinance for income-source. This protection is not listed within Fair Housing, however, may be considered a protected class within your locale. You should do the research BEFORE creating the policies and procedures of your rental property to ensure you are not violating the law by not accepting applicants with housing vouchers. Also, to ensure that you are clear of the process before acceptance or denial.

Myth Busting

For almost 20 years, I have worked with housing voucher recipients with my portfolio and for properties I manage for others. I have found that busting the myths around participants of the programs has opened the doors for profits and long-term occupancy. Here are the top 3 myths of Housing Voucher recipients and my take on each:

"They" will destroy your property.

Tenants come in all shapes, sizes, income groups, and professions. In my experience, there has not been any gauge to identifying an applicant as being better equipped to maintain a property than another. Be clear, that just because somebody has great credit, a good job, a clean criminal and eviction history, and makes a decent income does not equate to them being able or willing to take care of your house.

Proper and consistent screening as discussed later in the book, will help create a streamlined selection process for tenants and certainly can include verification of living conditions of the applicant(s) current and previous residences. Note that most administrators of housing vouchers have a process for transitioning residents which includes a current landlord's letter of good standing.

As well, my experience reflects that Housing Vouching recipients stay for longer terms, with my company's average being 5-7 years. There have been several voucher recipients with a residency of over 15 years. With that said, even minor damage, because of long-term wear and tear, is well worth exploring subsidy housing as an option for your rental.

"They" bring high crime and nuisances.

To secure a housing voucher there are qualifications just as the ones you shall create in the application process. With that said, the program does background checks, and many Housing Voucher recipients have no criminal history. Furthermore, criminal activity is a sure way to have a voucher terminated along with evictions, complaints, or housing violations. It is less likely that a recipient would engage in such activity or allow it as it could jeopardize their family's housing, not just in your home but future homes they lease, as well.

"They" will not remain in the home and will leave owing rent.

Housing vouchers provide tenant's opportunities to secure housing outside of communities that may be plagued with drugs, gangs, and other negative influences. Vouchers provide a pathway to remove themselves and their families into better locations.

For landlords, turnover and vacancy is the biggest expense as discussed earlier and especially if not carefully managed and controlled, if having a housing voucher tenant can turnovers and vacancies you can keep the commitment to the "expense" pledge by intentionally minimizing costs with leasing to those that have a record of longer rental terms. Your bottom line will appreciate consistent cash flow.

Face facts. Residents that have excellent credit and higher incomes have more options and remaining in your rental home for 5-7 years is not as likely as it would be for one with fewer options and the ability to afford a greater array of housing choices.

With the above myth-busting, make it a point to dig deeper into accepting subsidies based on the profitability and not your perceptions.

Municipalities that offer housing choice vouchers have offices that can help walk you through the process and understand the procedures. In fact, due to the need for affordable housing, there is likely to be a regularly offered class or information session for new landlords. Note that every program may have a variety of processes and it is in your best interest to learn directly from the office that your property may qualify.

In almost 20 years, I have yet to experience any situation that is limited to those of a housing voucher recipient. Oddly, I have advocated for the program as I have found that the program's process and procedures have provided me, as a landlord and property manager, added layover of oversight. This includes the one-time monthly payments, annual inspections of the property, incentives for adding a home to the program and for vacancies as well as a "big brother" to contact when there are any challenges.

You may find that being open to the program and its participants can be a true game-changer in your buy-and-hold strategy.

CHAPTER VIII

SCREENING PROCESS: CREDIT, CRIMINAL, INCOME TO HOUSING RATIO, VERIFICATION OF INCOME, RENTAL HISTORY

Being legally choosy about prospective tenants is essential as you do not want your investment property to sit idle. You also don't want tenants who end up breaking the rules or their lease. Of course, you can't discriminate against people, but running credit checks, verifying income, and contacting references are all_legal and necessary ways to screen prospective tenants.

You can also include specific terms in your_rental agreement that specify each party's responsibilities. You can mitigate concerns by implementing The Three C's.

The Three C's of Tenant Screening

The value of properly screening potential tenants is immeasurable. It's not simply a measure to keep out the riffraff. Doing your due diligence to screen a prospective resident can make or break you in the rental industry for several reasons. Some of which are:

- **Credit:** Life happens, and people's credit scores may fluctuate. That said, there is no getting around the fact that a low credit score, and/or an unstable credit history demonstrates a likely inability to stay current with rent payments.

- **Criminal History:** Again, life happens and some even advise to disallow even the smallest offense. Here is where you can have built-in protocols for what to allow and disallow. For the safety of your other tenants and the surrounding neighborhood, a criminal background check is a must. At least evaluate whom to lease to, with a criminal history, on a case-by-case basis.

- **Consistency:** Rental history is an absolute must. NO EXCEPTIONS! Tenants lived somewhere before considering your property as their next home. What should be of concern to you and looked further into, is how many places they have lived and their rate of turnover. They could have excellent credit, and a background as pure as the undriven snow but every year—or even worse, shorter than a normal term of the lease—they change addresses. I have said once or twice in the book that, but it bears repeating...life happens. Now, they could have valid reasons for every move they have made, but their reasons are not as important as the frequency with which life happened to them. In other words, if consistent long-term occupancy is your goal, then a prospective tenant that will be gone after one lease term is not the optimal candidate.

Verifying residential history—Essential questions to ask

Would you re-rent to this tenant? Has the tenant ever been late? Are there any known damages?

Are there any known damages to your property, attributed to this tenant's responsibility?

If you did not do your due diligence, then you'll always ask yourself, "How did I contribute to this situation?" But, if you have asked these pertinent questions and the answer came back favorably, yet you now need a new carpet, new drywall, HVAC because filters were never changed, then that's just that person and you can't mediate that. There is nothing you can do if that's the person that walked into your property.

Military Affidavit Story (NC requirement): Why NOT screening kept a tenant in longer than necessary

I had an owner that came to me without screening their tenant. The tenant simply had cash, and I honestly do not know why that does not scare some landlords or property managers. It truly scares me when people say, "I have cash," as if the cash should negate the fact that they have no job or inadequate income. Some of the most telltale red flags are: if their residential history is shaky, if they are going through an eviction right now, if they have a criminal background and if they have a low credit score.

Stop, look, and listen when a potential tenant says, "I have cash," and they want to skip all the other background criteria in your usual application process. Most people actively trying to support themselves are excited to say, "Oh, I have a great job. I've been on my job for five years. I have a solid residential history. I've been with this company for four years. I just want to move because I need a bigger place."

That was not the case with this story. This property owner accepted someone at face value because they said they had cash. They allowed them to move in...to THEIR property. The tenant was paying on time for a while and then there was a hiccup.

In the state of North Carolina, we now have an additional step that you must take to do a summary ejectment or evict someone, which is our military affidavit. The military affidavit requires that this person is not in the military at the time that we are completing the eviction. There's only a couple of ways that you can prove this. You can either ask the tenant and have it in writing or some documentation saying that they are currently not in the military.

You can do an affidavit yourself, verifying that you have asked them this question, and this is their response. There is a search engine in which you can enter qualifying information to get the results on an individual's military status. The qualifying information is social security number, birth date, or full name; all information one should get in a normal vetting or application process. When you plug this information into a website given by the U.S. government, the search engine will report whether this person is currently active in the military.

The landlord, in this case, could not provide the information because they did not have it. The landlord did not have this information because they never collected the information from the tenant. They just let the person move in because they had cash.

Please know that every state can be different when it comes to eviction procedures. That is why it is so important to understand what your requirements are, for leasing and eviction, in the state in which your property is. What is the requirement for an eviction? We haven't had this for long in the state of North Carolina, however, it is a requirement.

So, if you were unaware of this law and process, then you go to court thinking you're going to do an eviction, it will surely surprise you when the Magistrate or Judge says, "Sorry Landlord, you need X-form, and we cannot proceed." Again, to accurately get the report that you need, you simply must have qualifying information. If you don't have qualifying information, you can't get it. The landlord came to me and said, "Hey, I'm having issues with this tenant. I would like for the tenant to stay. I don't necessarily want them to go, but I can't seem to evict them."

Of course, we reached out to the tenant in an effort to communicate and try to get them to pay. I discovered that the landlord never did an application. They never sat down and wrote an application out. They did have a lease in place, but he never collected any information on the tenant.

He did not conduct any screening regarding this person. Nothing was done. He, therefore, had a challenge with getting the tenant out. We ultimately had to groom this tenant, get this tenant to come in and give us all their data information, fill out what we call a resident data form so that we now have enough information, to evict him. That process took about three months.

Had the landlord followed an application process, this could have been resolved in a matter of weeks. We cannot be surprised when a tenant stops paying rent if we did not verify that they could pay rent to begin with. I have denied applicants who offered to pay cash for a long period of time because of their application. You should not negate screening a tenant, implementing whatever your processes or procedures are going to be because someone has cash. Never not screen someone.

You should never avoid screening. I recommend having an application in place for use with your mom, your cousin, your best friend, your coworker, and certainly for a stranger. I recommend that you create and consistently implement guidelines for screening a client. Every. Single. Time.

I have a seven-parameter system for screening tenants. You wouldn't lose a potentially great tenant, and you wouldn't burden yourself with a problem tenant, either. If you are new to being a landlord many things that I advise of, if not learned before you buy your property, will be learned over time. There are apps and software you can buy to aid in your screening of tenants. There are also companies, online or brick and mortar, which you can hire for this specific purpose. Until you are up to speed with the ins and outs of rental property management, a good rule of thumb is to ask those in the know.

In this instance, that would be a professional that specializes in property management. A consult with a professional is worth the cost of future mistakes.

The Dating Game – Why is building a relationship with your tenant so important?

Relationships matter. You are managing your landlord-tenant relationship just as much as the property.

Relationships with the tenant matter because 1. Going in the door, you are setting the precedent on how the process should work. You are making it very clear to the tenant where you stand as the landlord, in face-to-face communication with them, of course, but also in writing. 2. You are building rapport. That matters. I don't think that you need to be "besties," but I think that the tenant needs to understand your position and your role, even as the owner/landlord, in the process. Often, that also opens the door for clear communication from the tenant so that when anything is going on, they feel comfortable with approaching you. If you are so stern and so strict... unapproachable, they don't want to call you and tell you that there is maybe a maintenance issue going on, it can be problematic on many levels. They figure, hey, we'll just deal with it ourselves, or they figure they won't deal with it and just let it be until they leave.

If the relationship is not there, when issues arise where maybe they can't pay rent, they don't want to call you. They're embarrassed. They're possibly stressed. They want to run and hide from you when relationships and rapport have not been fostered. But, if you set up a good line of communication at the beginning, it's just a respectful thing.

They respect that you are the owner, you are the landlord, you're managing this property, and they can connect with you on the things that are important and if there is a challenge looming on the horizon.

From your perspective, you are also setting up that you expect to be respected as the landlord. And, that this is your property and that you have a set of processes and procedures that you not only want but require the tenant to follow. However, you're open enough to understand that there's some human element going on.

You want to make sure that anything that comes up, they feel comfortable with having a conversation with you. Whether you can deal with it based on your processes and procedures, that's another subject, but at least both parties have mutual respect for the respective positions at play, in the relationship. I think that's key, more so when there are issues that arise, than just the day-to-day.

Keys to Keeping Your Tenants Happy

Keeping your tenants happy will result in more on-time rental payments and proper care and maintenance of your rental property. Turnover is expensive and so are repairs. Getting your property ready to rent, advertising the vacancy, showing the property, and screening tenants are some of the most costly and labor-intensive tasks involved in owning and profiting from a rental property.

Once you have found an ideal tenant, retention of that renter will become an important aspect of your business. Below are some "keys" to accomplish this:

1. **Prompt Attention to Inquiries, Repairs, and Complaints**

   Maintenance requests are particularly important. No matter how great your tenants are, appliances break, faucets leak, and general wear and tear happen. Your tenants will feel valued when you promptly respond to their needs, and they are more likely to care for the property when they see how you respond. Landlords who are slow or non-responsive to maintenance requests are a major cause of tenant turnover.

   While some investors choose to self-manage, hiring a property manager can save you a lot of time and keep your tenants happy. With years of experience behind us, property managers know how to handle a wide range of urgent calls and routine maintenance requests with ease.

2. **Offer an Online Tenant Portal**

   Offering the convenience of an online tenant portal where renters can make online payments and request maintenance support is huge and most Millennials and other renters expect it, now.

Be fair. When it comes to rent increases, keeping rent within the local market rate and giving prior notice to tenants is important when trying to keep your tenants happy. Good quality tenants are hard to come by. Be fair and it will be appreciated and valued by your tenants.

3. **Look After the Property and Your Tenants**
   Your job does not end with handing over the keys to the rental property. To attract and retain good tenants, you must maintain a clean, well-attended property that demonstrates your intentions as a landlord. You need to make your tenants feel happy and proud that they are living there. An overgrown landscape or malfunctioning appliances are factors that will count against you in terms of tenant happiness. A landlord that maintains a clean and well-kept property and shows concern for the comfort and well-being of their tenants, wins their support and loyalty which results in a winning situation for all.

Setting the Standard—Tenant Handbook, Orientation on Processes

It is just something about HVAC systems, weekends, and holidays.

If there is any maintenance request, I can count on being submitted at an odd time, it is an HVAC unit. It appears systems decide to go completely out when I am either on vacation, at a family cookout, or in a deep sleep. I recently had a tenant whose AC went out during a holiday. Though my office did its absolute best to explain the warranty process before moving in the tenant, our office had to recap on multiple occasions during the repair process.

If you are unfamiliar with warranty claims, below is a "rough idea" of the flow:

- The landlord calls in or submits the warranty claim, online.

- The warranty company assigns a vendor.

- The vendor then contacts the landlord or the tenant directly, to schedule service.

- The vendor follows their home warranty processes and procedures to get the diagnosis and gain approval for a repair.

- Vendor may have to order parts and come back to do the maintenance.

That is generally how the process works and if you elect to have this type of service, your tenant should know prior to the process not during a conversation while you are on the beach and they are sitting in a very HOT home in the summer or extremely COLD home in the winter, especially when they assume that all they needed to do is report the issue and have it immediately fixed.

In our case, the tenant did make a complaint about the AC not working. We did get someone out on a holiday. It was a struggle, having them understand that it was not a matter that we could just pick up the phone to call someone and have them go out and we reiterated our process that was made clear during our resident orientation.

Landlords must ensure residents understand what the process looks like and provide a clear idea of a likely timeline for resolution on any issue specifically maintenance.

So, in this case we did have to explain to the tenant that it could take longer. It could take three days to get on the maintenance schedule. We got over that. Once that tech went out to the property, they realized that there was a part that needed to be ordered. They got approval for the part. However, the landlord did not immediately want to do any concessions for the tenant that would allow the tenant to either order or have HVAC units put in the house, such as window units or standup units, or of course, to allow the tenant to go to a hotel.

That's a challenge because the owner does not manage the property on a day-to-day basis. So, the owner is not the one getting the phone calls every hour trying to figure out what is going on with the HVAC. My recommendation to landlords is become educate on what is considered emergencies per the law and use good communication to help the resident understand not only the requirements but the process the landlord is taking to resolve the issue. Education and communication are key.

However, there are some things that would have made this situation easier for all, either securing temporary rental AC or allowing the tenant to purchase temporary cooling systems and providing a reimbursement. The owner decided to allow a $100 allowance for rental units. The situation was a challenge because as the property manager, I had to go back and explain the owner's position to the tenant without any flexibility.

Can you imagine the conflict that comes with an email to a tenant saying, "I'm only going to give you $100 to cool your nearly 3000 square foot house, for a total of three weeks?" Do you believe that $100 is enough to physically cool off a three-story, 3000 square foot home, with four bedrooms? Is it feasible?

Really think about that.

This is an example of why it is important that there be a process and procedure in place for maintenance issues outlining how maintenance should be handled. If you are open as a landlord to hear and listen to the other person's side, you will see the savings from tenant satisfaction and longevity and have peace of mind from a more seamless process when troubles arise.

It boils down to communication and an issue of respect and empathy. The thought could be, "My tenant won't leave." Maybe she will, maybe she won't. Why risk it? Right? Why risk that the next month they are going to pay late? Why risk allowing "anything" happening versus spending the $400 it would take to get at least four units in the property temporarily?

That is a dilemma that you will face, more than once as a landlord. To clarify, I'm not saying be irrational, like giving in to a "Put me up in a hotel" request when it's 72 degrees outside. That should not happen either. But, when two parties have good communication have clear processes and procedures in place, and expectations set with one another it is much easier to work out a solution or compromise. The goal is where everyone can walk away satisfied and with the landlord-tenant relationship unharmed.

When you do not have that, then it's harder. Sometimes it's harder when you only have written communication because we all know people can take words out of context. However, if you are talking to your tenant and they can hear your voice, they can hear empathy and sincerity in your voice, in your conversation, then they are more likely to accept a "meet me halfway" solution and let go of the "give me what I want or I'm walking" mindset.

This is the challenge of being a landlord. You either feel the need to "put your foot down" so hard that it's practically audible or you're up in the air and let your tenant dictate the outcome to keep them happy. Good communication between both parties helps with this challenge. Also, for the communication to be a vehicle to avoid conflict, you can't encourage communication and consistency from your tenant but not practice what you preach.

Before You Raise the Rent...

I hear it every day, across many industries. Prices are being raised because of the economy. My prices for...EVERYTHING is being raised, therefore the prices I charge for my goods and services must, too, be raised. It is a fact of life and very common in business. Investing in real estate is not just retirement security, or a means to make ends meet. Whether you have 1 or 100 properties, real estate investment is a business. With all of that in mind, the raising of rent must be done with great thought and analysis, if at all.

"If at all?" Yes, if at all. Your market may not favor a raising of rent, for current or even prospective tenants. Some investors will raise rent every year, at lease renewal time, for their current residents. This accomplishes two things: sets a precedent for the possibility of a rent increase and, since word-of-mouth is such a powerful tool, that same precedent that is set for current tenants lays the groundwork for prospective tenants to know that rent increases are always a possibility.

The "annual rent increase" methodology is a matter of degrees. The need for rentals is constant and therefore demand is high. In these situations, you must remain competitive while trying to stay profitable. Just because the demand is high, do not forget the supply can be also. Make your increases fit with what your local market can handle.

There are 3 things you should remember when considering a rent increase:

Affordability. Your first consideration should be local housing affordability. This can easily be obtained through a local property management company or Realtor. They can advise of fair market rents in a particular area. Remember, rents can only rise until affordability (what potential renters can/will pay in your area) peaks. Affordability is right when a monthly rent is approximately a third of the median take-home pay for a household.

Once it rises above this point investors are likely to experience vacancies and/or late rent payments, as affordability has peaked. Another great tool is Rent-o-Meter. This is a tool that will tell you what other homes have recently rented for in your area. (Also, this tool is a great asset when buying property to make sure your anticipated rents are in line with the market.)

Availability. One thing to never forget when investing in real estate is that what is happening in one area or market cannot be applied to all markets. Some larger cities can build and build and build and seem to always have a bottomless pool of potential renters.

A good way to gauge if your market indicates favorability of rent increase is to monitor building permit activity. If the market is saturated, maintaining occupancy is more important than raising the rent. If you need help with this, consult a professional. Remember, a consult fee is always better than the expenses of inexperience.

Renter-to-Population Ratio. This concept can be thought of as a haven for investors. In this circumstance, the landlord is holding all the cards. An invaluable source to discern your area's renter ratio is an interactive map provided by the U.S. Department of Commerce. When you know that there is a surplus of renters, you can decide if a rent increase is feasible or ill-advised.

Do not raise rents arbitrarily and when it's contraindicated. There is a saying, "Pigs get fat, and hogs get slaughtered." Eloquent, right? Simply put, don't get greedy!

When an area has a larger ratio, adjust rent, not only according to your cost-benefit analysis but also when and if the market can bear it. Whether a little or a lot, an improper increase may prompt tenants, current and future, to compare your rental against all others. If your increase was not dictated by the market, you may lose the comparison and in turn, your renter, creating an unnecessary turnover, remarketing, and vacancy costs.

CHAPTER IX

EVICTIONS

One of the most challenging parts of being a landlord is handling an eviction. It can be stressful for tenants and landlords. Someone has had a difficult situation arise that has prevented them from paying rent or paying in a timely fashion and the result of this is landing both parties in court.

Tenant Withholding Rent Leads To Eviction

I have not experienced a tenant being justified for withholding rent however my time spent in courtrooms listening to cases, I have seen where tenants have been justified. For instance, someone not having a stove for three months. And, in such cases, the official justification is going to come through the court system. What has happened is the person has withheld rent and the owner now wishes to evict that person.

During court, it comes out that the tenant has withheld the rent, which is not right. You can't arbitrarily withhold rent. I want to make sure that is clear. Oh, I forgot. I'm talking to them. (It can get confusing, as I have represented parties on every side of the eviction equation.)

So, what happened is that the judge then said, "Yes. There is a summary ejectment that can take place here because the tenant did not pay their rent. They owe you $3,000. However, as the magistrate, I am going to say that they're going to get a credit of $2,000 because you did not give them a stove for three months." I could not determine the justification, but a magistrate certainly can determine whether the person is justified in withholding the rent.

When it has been determined that the scenario warrants eviction, it is still not that simple. There is a process. It can vary from state to state. If you happen to be reading this, somewhere in the world besides North Carolina, be advised that it is a good basis for many things, but you need to know your local laws and regulations and govern yourself accordingly.

The following is a brief overview of the eviction process my firm completes. Note you must follow your state and local laws to initiate and complete an eviction.

10 Day Notice

When we file an eviction in North Carolina, we must give the tenant a 10 Day Notice. In our office, the 10 Day Notice is already in the lease, so we can waive that notice requirement. Make sure your lease is legally vetted to ensure you under your lease requirements when giving notices.

Court Date

Once we file the eviction with the Clerk of the Court, we will have 10-14 days before our first court date based on the court calendar. On the day of court, the tenant has the opportunity to present their situation and explain why rent has not been paid. We almost always gain possession of the property. We then need to allow the tenants 10 days to vacate or to reach an agreement, in our office, this may allow the tenant to stay in the property after paying all outstanding balances.

Writ of Possession

If the tenant is unable to make payment arrangements with us and they still do not vacate the property, we will need to file a Writ of Possession. This is often referred to as the padlocking process, and it is extremely humiliating to the tenant and adds stress to the landlord. The sheriff comes out and assesses the property to determine whether the tenants are still there. The sheriff will ask the tenants to vacate or determine that the tenants have left and can decide what to do with any possessions that might be left behind in the property.

Timelines

The eviction process can take between 30 days to months, depending on the county and state. It is stressful for the owner because they have not received their rental funds yet still need to make mortgage payments. They also worry about the property and whether any damage will be found. It can take some time to turn the property over and get it ready for a new tenant.

It is our goal as property managers to make evictions smooth. When we have landlords, who work with us and immediately respond to our need to do an eviction, the process is easier. We also communicate with tenants and provide resources that can help them pay the rent and refer them to other companies that may help them find less expensive housing. This is a win/win for everyone because the tenant feels supported and the landlord knows we are doing our best to get an individual out of the property when rent cannot be paid.

If you have any questions about the eviction process, please refer to your attorney to ensure you are proceeding properly in accordance with the law and your lease.

Tenant/Landlord Disputes:

Tenant Caused Maintenance Issues. The language of the lease is very important in the relationship between you as landlord/owner and the tenant. Questions are answered, policies are outlined, and consequences are defined in how a proper lease agreement is composed. Two vital areas that are covered in the lease language are maintenance policies, handling, responsibilities, and the handling of nonpayment of rent.

The tenant in question may be a little lax when it comes to reading the lease before signing. BIG MISTAKE on their part but can cause problems from the landlord/property manager perspective, also. If possible and to mitigate subsequent issues that may arise, best practices dictate that you stress that the entire lease is read to the point of complete understanding, before signing.

As a landlord, you have a lot Invested into each transaction regarding your property. As a PM, your success is tied into not only the longevity of each tenant's residency but to as seamless a tenure as possible. There are too many scenarios that will threaten a "seamless tenure" when the tenant does not read AND UNDERSTAND the language of their lease, how maintenance issues are handled, what their responsibilities are, and how things are handled from the landlord/PM side.

Whatever you can do to convey that this is not just your residence for the next X number of months. This is their landlord's property. They have a lot invested in it. Money, energy, and lots of time. Time that includes covering how every aspect of you leasing their property should be handled. The least they can do is read before signing.

The schedule of maintenance is generally well outlined in a lease. Point out any information about the schedule of when tenants can expect contractors to come to handle certain things, routinely. You may also want to outline what things tenants are expected to do, routinely/regularly, to keep the home and the functions therein, running smoothly to the benefit of all concerned.

The tenant/landlord relationship will be threatened at the onset when the tenant does not read the lease as closely as possible. Just imagine the communication, even though the handling of the scenario was specifically outlined when there is a maintenance issue that is the tenant's fault? However, since they are "just renting" they fail to realize it is their responsibility.

Now, some leases will read, that while it was their fault, it is not their responsibility. Then, there are others that will advise, in detail, how if maintenance issues arise that are not part of normal wear and tear, it is the responsibility of the tenant to resolve. This usually means that there are outsourced contractors used (the property's maintenance men, or subcontractors), and when it's resolved, the tenant is billed.

The impact to the tenant is up to you as the landlord and the severity is likely on a case-by-case basis, depending on the cost of the repair. Whatever is determined to be the severity or cost, the impact is usually the transfer of the cost to the tenant, refusing to renew the lease, immediate eviction, and/or negative rating for future leases with other properties.

Before you put someone in for eviction, make sure that there are no pending issues that could come back and bite you. For instance:

- not having a stove if required by your state law

- having major plumbing issues

- lack of a working heating system in the winter

- no running water in kitchen or bath

So, before you file a summary ejectment for someone that you know is withholding rent based on any kind of a delayed repair or maintenance issue, I would say look to have that resolved. The magistrate or the judge, depending on what jurisdiction you're in, is going to be the end all be all. When you've not done your due diligence or kept your end of the bargain (followed terms of your lease), you waste energy, time, and money because everything will come out and not likely fall in your favor.

I considered adding some of my more enlightening and remarkable court chronicles in this book. Stories that would encompass going to court and avoiding court and everything in between. I've seen a lot of interesting things in court over 15 years, some very interesting, funny things. But I'll save that for another time.

KEYS TO PROPERTY PRESERVATION

CHAPTER X

PROPERTY PRESERVATION

Plan Financially for Turn-Key Processes

The turning process does not have to be painful and it is something that a landlord should anticipate over the life of a rental property. If a tenant has lived in your home for five to seven years, you should plan for a substantial "turn" before a new tenant can move in. One way to mitigate your expenses is by doing some work yourself or having a great team.

This is one of the reasons that "building a team" is part of the initial process of preparing to invest in rental property. An 1,800 square foot home should not cost you $10,000 to paint. Painting an 1,800 square foot, two-story rental house could cost you maybe $1,800 to $2,400 if you shop for vendors and build relationships. However, you may now know this until you shop around for pricing and/or build relationships with vendors for repeat business.

It is helpful to educate yourself on common repair costs, such as:

- What's the average cost of repainting my house?
- What's the average cost per square foot of installing a basic carpet on my property?
- What's the average cost of having to repair or replace granite?
- What's my 3–5-year plan for maintenance or upgrades?

These are some of the costs that owners should consider when planning and budgeting for turnkey services. You never know how you're going to get the property back from a tenant. However, preparation and the anticipation of costs can make these challenges more manageable.

CHAPTER XI

KNOW EVERY INCH
OF YOUR PROPERTY

From Day 1, no matter how your property management journey begins, get to know all aspects of your property. Basic property characteristics that you should know, include:

- How many square feet is the property?

- Year Built? (Effective date if major renovations have been completed)

- What are the utilities on your property? Do you have a gas water heater? Do you have a gas fireplace? How is your heat operated? Is your stove electric? Is there an option for gas appliances if currently electric?

- What size are your blinds?

- What type of lighting do you have?

- Do you have copper piping?

- How many rooms do you have in your house? How are they designated and the square footage of each?

- Be sure to write down serial numbers and the age of appliances and systems.

Have a set place where you store information regarding your property and revisit it for the purposes of documenting the property. Build a list of vendors that you can use to help preserve your property: HVAC tech, plumber, electrician, an appliance tech, general contractors are a few. As issues arise and your experience increases, you may add to that list, as your business dictates. My list is not inclusive, as every real estate investment company is different. My purpose is to show that you need to have key people in place to operate in their realm of expertise so that your investment journey runs a little more smoothly.

Repairs, general upkeep, and major repairs are a part of real estate investing. It is just part of the equation. Realizing that proper planning for it and acting when the need is realized, could be the difference in making profits and losing money. You can very easily pour everything that you have earned to do repairs after the fact, that a successful landlord planned for, preemptively.

The top, most common repairs an owner might make in a five-year span are:

- Garbage disposal

- Oven element replacement

- HVAC (one of the three C's is the condenser, capacitor, and coil)

- Water heater

- Wax ring on toilets

- Minor roof leaks

- Plumbing lines

Recommendations for periodic preventative maintenance are:

- Flushing your plumbing lines

- Pressure washing and cleaning gutter

- Trimming back trees from the house and monitoring growing tree roots

- Inspecting both the attic and crawl space

- Cleaning out the HVAC duct work

Note that the above items can be helpful and easily budgeted over a period of time.

If you have a home warranty on your property, preventive maintenance may be required to ensure service requests are approved.

Pre-purchase or Pre-Rental Ready Inspection

A pre-purchase or pre-market ready inspection will be an inspection of the full property. If you have just purchased or acquired a property and you have not inspected it, I recommend a certified home inspection of all vital systems (plumbing, mechanical, HVAC, etc.) before a tenant moves in.

My recommendation is to do this every three to five years on your property so that you can have a detailed overview of everything about the condition of your property. When was the last time you looked at your fireplace? Have you had the chimney checked? If no one ever uses it, how do you know if something is going on with it, and has potentially become hazardous until that one person wants to use it and they can't?

Regarding roofing, even with a professional property manager, they're not going to do your roof inspection. Roof inspections are something that a home inspector would do along with every other component in the house. You might have a room that nobody in the home uses and all the electrical outlets are out. A home inspector will help to determine the maintenance immediately required. I do recommend at least having a true home inspection at least every three to five years, or if the tenant has lived in the property for three to five years, once that tenant moves out to get that full inspection done.

Bi-Annual Evaluations

My recommendation is for owners to do small things that ensure their asset is protected. One way to protect the property is with home inspections. Many clients ask their property managers to do a simple walk-through of the property. That's great to get a look at how the tenant is caring for the house. However, a true home inspection is important to get to the bones and the meat of a property. An inspector can check for roof leaks and potential plumbing issues. These things are probably not caused by tenants, but to an individual just doing a walk-through, these problems can go unseen.

If you look at the definition for an inspection, a professional inspection is much more in-depth than an evaluation. An evaluation is when someone just comes by and kind of peruses or walks through a house with an "eye test". They evaluate what they can see on the surface. "Oh, the carpets are dirty. There's a hole in the wall. The house is clean. It looks great." That is an evaluation and sometimes, all that is required.

You may walk into a house, and it looks great cosmetically, but there can be challenges or issues that are unseen. A certified inspector is going to check the voltage on your outlets. They are going to check the fireplace and the roof. They are going to check the HVAC and confirm if it is cooling the way it should. An evaluation may only check to make sure it turns on with a change of the thermostat.

An inspection verifies that it is not just cooling the house but performing the way it should with the expected output.

An inspection or a professional inspection is going to allow someone to come into the property to check, what I call "the bones" of the property, the appliances, the systems of the property, to ensure that everything is working as it should. And, if it's not, it's going to then result in you calling in a professional contractor or a licensed technician to further evaluate what has been found.

In other words, you probably should be doing consistent evaluations of the property. Then plan to have a professional, true inspection of the property every three to five years, which generally is from top to bottom; unless you decide that you do not want certain aspects of the inspection. Your choice but also your responsibility.

However, if you are doing an annual inspection, whether it's a self-inspection which allows the tenant to send you documentation of the home based on your parameters—or, if you're just doing a walkthrough of the property or even if it's every three months or if it's every six months—remember this is your house, you can set it up however you want.

If you are doing that, what you might want to do is mitigate how much loss is done. If you go to the house the first time, our recommendation if you're a novice landlord is that you have a move-in inspection with your tenant. You complete the move-in inspection, or they complete the move-in inspection. You handle any issues that need to be handled, upfront and proactively. You document any things that need to be documented. And, then about 30 days after they move in, you ask for the opportunity to go to the property just to do a walkthrough.

This is to make sure everything is okay and explain some things that they did not know, during the move-in process. It is meant to be very friendly and starts the "relationship" building I'd previously recommended. The goal is for it to be very friendly, very genuine, and set a precedent for your attention to their concerns and the steps you will continue to take for the preservation of your property. It will also give insight into how the person is setting your house up.

The process can give you a lot of necessary information about the tenant and how their time in the rental may go. They moved in, all the boxes are out the way, they've gotten everything in the kitchen, they put up some things. This can give you an idea of how this person may live. Could that change? Of course, it could. The likelihood that it's going to drastically change is probably not there. However, it does happen.

I followed that same process in my third house which happened to be, at the time, our primary residence. When we moved out of it, we bought a new house. We obtained a great tenant through diligent screening. That person, however, only stayed six months. They had to move for work. So, we were devastated because they were great tenants. Everything about them was just perfect.

But we wound up getting a cool second tenant. No harm, no foul. When we contracted with the second tenant, there are some things that we didn't know when they first moved in, which we thought were odd. The tenant's mother co-signed for her. This was a middle-aged person, but the mom co-signed for her. She did have some children and it was our understanding that she was coming out of a difficult situation, but the mom wanted to make sure she was safe and sound. Her application came back great. Everything about the actual applicant indicated there were no issues.

They moved in. We did exactly what I advise of my clients. We did a move-in inspection. The house was immaculate! With three little kids, not to say that that's an issue, but when I'm saying there wasn't a toy...nothing was out or out of place. It was just an immaculate property. We, of course, got comfortable with this tenant. I got comfortable with this tenant. She would allow us to come in with no problem, whatsoever. So, the first three, four years everything was cool. We came in, as needed. The same with vendors. No problem.

Within approximately the last 12 to 18 months of her occupancy, something changed. We couldn't go in. The outside still looked okay, but we couldn't go in. We started to get calls from the neighbors about our property. Just different things.

When it was time to do walkthroughs, it seemed like we were always getting excuses. Even with some vendors doing maintenance, it was always an excuse on why we could not get into the property. Finally, I said, "Look, we're coming down. It has been almost a year now. We must evaluate the property. We need to come into the property."

What we found was probably the worst or possibly second worst experience that I have had with a tenant. This situation was within the top five! At some point, the tenant had become a hoarder. And, it had to have happened within the year and a half. In every inch of the house, there was something. Every single inch. Even the garage was full, from top to bottom of just...stuff.

I have no idea how the person even maneuvered inside of that house. It was just... I don't even understand. It went from a model home to made for cable TV hoarding program, in just a relatively short period of time. That is why I recommend people do inspections, frequently, just to get an understanding of what is going on and to know that things can change. It doesn't have to always be. Even if a tenant is challenging at the beginning, with some coaching, things can change. Conversely, they can start off as a perfect tenant but by the end of the day, unchecked, your property can be absolutely TRASHED!

It was just the craziest thing. I had never seen anything like it in my career. And, to this day, I've never seen anything like it since. It literally looked like what you see on TV.

We did reach out and discovered there were some mental challenges that factored into our end result. Believe it or not, we didn't evict her. I remember she moved on her own, but we did give a notice. They didn't owe any rent. And, surprisingly, we didn't have any pest issues or anything like that. The person just had started collecting stuff and they just kept on collecting.

The moral of that story is tenants can start out one way, good or bad, and change. You just never know.

"That Gut Feeling" Evaluations

I have a landlord that had a long-term tenant. The tenant had been living in their home for around six years and residing alone when they moved into the property. The landlord had started to do inspections in the early years however, over time, they stopped inspecting or visiting the property as regularly as they should.

The tenant sent an email to the landlord stating their desire to vacate. This happened to be around Christmas time. The owner notified the tenant that they had a notice requirement. Then, suddenly, the tenant changed their mind. They suddenly did not need to move any longer, which seemed a little odd. (You can't afford to ignore these red flags. Err on the side of caution and if you don't investigate, at least stay aware of "odd" or different behavior.) The rent started coming in just a little bit slower. The person had been paying on time for years, but the rent started coming in late after the vacate/not vacate situation.

Finally, by May, the tenant sent an email saying that they were truly going to vacate this time, and they would be out within 60 days. By the time the tenant vacated in the fall, the entire house had been destroyed by pets. Apparently, the tenant had vacated when he initially submitted the previous request. However, they left their family members on the property. Their family members let their pets have at it, for some reason. In my 20 years, I've never had to replace sub-floors in a rental property. The home reeked in nearly every room of this four-bedroom house.

In retrospect, the owner thought to himself, "We should have gone by more often." As a landlord, an individual landlord (only having one or two properties), you can control how evaluations are managed. Even if you want to go by the property every day, that's your choice.

I highly recommend coming up with a process and routine, that allows you to evaluate or visit the property on a regular basis. Even if it's just for an air filter check. This would get you into the property every 30 to 90 days.

If you are working remotely or living outside of the area of your investment, that can be a challenge. However, these days there are so many ways for you to automate a process. Contractors are looking for work all the time. Some inspectors can conduct these evaluations on your behalf. Property managers are offering à la carte services that can conduct inspections for you, as well.

I do believe that property preservation is about knowing your property. That should include ensuring that you have a process in place to check on your property frequently enough that you could spot the red flags of deterioration and abuse. It is imperative that you understand that you do not necessarily want to keep someone in your home, simply because they are paying the rent.

Think about this, if you are making a $200 a month profit, you don't want to turn around and spend the $10,000 (made over 5 years) just to rehab the house after it is destroyed due to the lack of timely or periodic evaluations. Because that's not a profit. Many issues that landlords uncover, after the fact (whether eviction or voluntarily vacating), could have been controlled or mitigated with periodic inspections.

Conducting Sporadic Drive-By's

A "drive-by," in real estate, basically means you just drive by the house to see what's going on. If you drive by the house and a car is parked in the yard and you're in a subdivision where that shouldn't be, that's a flag. That is a sign. If every blind in the house is cracked, that's a sign. If the yard is in disarray, that's a sign. If there's a lot of debris on the outside of the house, that's a sign. If you're getting HOA violations every single month for something, that is a major sign that you need to go into the property and assess how the tenants are caring for, or not caring for your property and determine if further action is required.

Monitoring Vacant Homes

Every year, our office closes for a week in December. In December of 2014, a customer came to us through an online realty search engine. Ordinarily, we do not personally show the property. Our office procedure is that when a potential tenant makes an inquiry about a property, we respond to them and request they send over a copy of their driver's license. They, then, receive a code to unlock and view our rental properties. This individual did exactly that.

Our office was scheduled to be closed from Christmas to the new year. The person called and asked to see the property. They called back to say that they loved it and would get back in touch with us. Great...no problem. We leave for vacation.

Our office policy is that we go and view our properties every 7 to 10 days, based on traffic, just to make sure that our tenants or properties are not having any issues.

We reopened on January 2nd. Our intern went out to check on this property and it just so happened we had two properties on the same street, four houses away from each other. We gave him the address, and when he got to the house, he called to say that "...there was no lockbox on the door."

My first thought was "Oh, we must have given him the wrong address." One property was located at house number 8714, and the other was 8730. I just assumed that I had given him 8730 and not 8714. He said, "No, ma'am. I got the right address, right house."

He came back to the office, got the key, and went into the property. Not only had somebody taken the lockbox, but the whole house was also furnished top to bottom. We are not just talking about a little bit of furniture. They had full home décor, with masks and candles hanging off the walls. This was a four-bedroom house. The dining room, kitchen, and the whole house was furnished as if they had been living there for 20 years.

They had mail coming to the house, and a bank statement was on the counter. Apparently, they had scoped out the house and heard us say that we were going on vacation. They moved into the house over Christmas break and settled in.

I told them they had to leave at that very moment. They either could leave, immediately or I was calling the police. They did manage to get their stuff out. Later, I found during a real estate class for property managers, that this phenomenon of sneaking into houses was an ongoing issue in Charlotte. Those perpetrators would move into a rental illegally with the goal of staying in the home for 30 days. If they made it to the 30-day mark, without being discovered, then the situation changes drastically. It's no longer a squatter problem, they would now be a tenant by law.

After 30 days of inhabiting a home, a squatter can take possession of the property. This brings up the matter of how do you maintain your property when it's not occupied?

Landlords that are marketing their home themselves should install an alarm system to maintain and secure an unoccupied property. Using electronic codes versus the lockboxes and Ring ® technology can be helpful in avoiding the "squatter phenomenon". Note, nobody thinks this situation could happen to them until it happens. Take this precaution that as a landlord you need to implement a strategy to monitor you home when occupied and vacant.

Handling General Maintenance Concerns

Most tenants treat the place in which they reside as if it is their property. However, there's always that one. Being a landlord entails more than the collection of rent checks. As a part of that carefully drafted lease agreement, include a property check-in schedule and then actually follow through. As the owner, you have the right to make sure your property is maintained. Protect your investment by ensuring tenants are respecting your investment.

Monitor Maintenance

One consideration for landlords is to evaluate how to manage and monitor maintenance requests? Do you have multiple maintenance orders for a broken handle for the refrigerator? Do you continue to get maintenance orders for the AC? Do you find similar damages when conducting your periodic property evaluations?

The lease agreement should lay out, in detail, what the tenant is responsible for. It should also advise them of any charges that would be deemed outside of normal wear and tear. And, you may have to do some research to figure out what your state considers normal wear and tear. State laws versus what you would want to include in your agreement are an important factor in how you write your agreement, what you can apply as tenant responsibility, and in many ways dictate the flow of the tenant/landlord relationship.

If you have a tenant in the property that you are communicating with and you are inspecting the property as you should, there is an opportunity for you to coach that tenant on how to return that property to you. Especially if they're wanting to continue to be on the property.

So, if you conduct an inspection and you see something wacky, communicate with that tenant what you've found and how correct an issue.

A common challenge for landlords is having residents regularly change the air filters. It would be simple to advise the resident on your inspection visit,

"Let me show you how to change these filters". And, with that teaching, leave them with a pack of 10 filters, making it easy for them to change and keep the system running at peak efficiency for you as the owner and them as the party responsible for the utilities.

Now, you've done your part in helping them. If they don't do it, then they're just not the person that's going to do it. Some just will never take on that level of accountability or responsibility. In a year if they don't do what you've advised is their responsibility and even provided them the knowledge and means to do so, don't renew that lease. You move on because you know that that is not the person that you're going to be able to assist or care for your property.

The Pitfalls of Deferred Repairs

When you become an investment property owner, but it's not "what you do," you'll quickly learn that things are different from maintaining your home. Being a landlord is an entirely different animal than simply being a homeowner.

One main difference between the two, and there are many, is the human factor. What you may resolve to live with cannot always be applied to another person. This can be true with another person within your own home, let alone someone who happens to be paying for residence on your property. That being the case, there are areas of the management of your rental property, that can't be treated in a "they'll get around to it" type of way.

One such area is the issue of maintenance and repairs. I have often said and reiterated that investing in income properties is not for the faint of heart. My clients know and you should, also, that it is far from just finding a renter and collecting rent. It is an investment and investments require your due diligence and attention. It's like a garden. Once you plant the seeds, to reap the rewards of a plentiful harvest, you must tend to it—water, maintain, and address what issues may arise.

Even if you have written in the language of your lease that much of the cosmetic maintenance is the responsibility of the tenant, there are other things that will solely fall on your shoulders. Not giving those things proper time and attention can lead to unnecessary headaches, problems, and costs.

One such unnecessary headache is the escalation of a minor issue to a catastrophe. Some subscribe to the school of thinking that if it's not a problem or not that big as of a problem now, then you're wasting money. (I do some preventative maintenance and then when it eventually needs repair, I pay for it again.) Well, that's just nonsensical.

Regular maintenance of certain home needs and the prompt maintenance of a new issue prevent a costly repair. Repair and maintenance are two different things. The former can all too often be a cost that hurts in a way that few novice landlords are prepared to absorb. Maintenance is an ongoing, proactive battle in property preservation.

Reputation. Your next renter may only come if the previous renter was satisfied. Depending on the size of your city, word of mouth can make or break you. Furthermore, depending on the surplus of the market and the widespread draw of social media to help make all of our decisions, you absolutely need renters that are leaving to be leaving with a positive experience to tweet, post, and talk about.

Someone who has encountered deferred repairs, a difficult reporting process, and a landlord that seems to be uncaring about what they are viewing as their home for the duration, will reflect in your ability or inability to secure new tenants.

Danger/Possible Litigation. Some repairs simply must be addressed immediately. The fact that it is something you feel that they can live with because it's something you could, simply won't fly when comes to being an investment property owner.

There haven't been 503 million lawyer television shows because people don't like to sue. And, add to this being a very litigious society, the previous bad experiences that a tenant might have had, may make them quick to pull the trigger when their safety and well-being are at risk due to things like loose floorboards and suspicious mold.

Even if you don't have a green thumb, I'm sure you understand the concept that you reap what you sow. Make your investment always bring forth a plentiful harvest, by addressing maintenance issues as they come. Even better, be proactive and address issues before they become problems. If it becomes overwhelming, invest further, by securing the services of a competent property management company. You'll be happy you did.

How to Prep the Home for Safety

I cannot stress enough the importance of preparing a rental home for safety. This could include providing safety mechanisms, ensuring that your smoke detectors work properly and that carbon monoxide detectors are in place. All your safety devices should be tested regularly.

HVAC filters are also a potential hazard. Making sure those filters get changed, so that there is no clog in the system will minimize costs in the long term. Also, ensuring that there is no debris around your water heater. The dryer vent is another hazard that many people neglect to maintain, specifically the cover on the outside.

Recently, I was performing a drive-by of a community. As I was driving by, I saw birds fly into the dryer vent on a two-story house. I immediately stopped my car as instinctively I wanted to warn the occupants. I didn't know the person at all, however, I knocked on the person's door.

The resident came to the door and said, "Yes, ma'am?" And I said, "I am so sorry to bother you. Here is my card with my name and who I am. I just wanted to let you know that I saw birds fly into your dryer vent, and that's a potential safety issue. I am a property manager and I just wanted to let you know in case you did not already." And, she said, "Thank you so much. I have reported this several times to my property manager and they haven't been out." And, I said, "I just want to let you know because the birds are inside your vent right now, which means there could be a nest inside there." Mind you this was extreme, but I did so because I know the danger this issue can pose.

So, my recommendation is to make sure that the dryer vents on your property are cleaned out and that your tenants do their part to ensure the laundry room vent access is clean and free of debris or storage items.

Emergency Repairs

Emergency repairs are things such as actively leaking water. Actively leaking water is water that cannot be stopped or requires a shut-off to be stopped. I think this is always important. You always want to know just in case any pipes have cracked. It's important because water causes so much damage, and unintended water causes more damage like mildew, mold, etc.

You should always want to deal with these types of issues, though minor to start, as an emergency. Electrical issues are also important because you never know what could come out of them. You certainly want to deal with any kind of potentially hazardous and costly electrical issues as soon as possible.

It's key to know how maintenance items are required by the law to be handled and if it must be done in a certain timeframe as the landlord. Because you don't want to be breaking laws by not having repairs done.

I believe the lack of understanding the law is probably one of the things that landlords miss managing their property. Many buy a property and don't have all the information about how to manage the property from a legal standpoint, They just place tenant in a property and figure out afterwards that there are applicable laws whether it's state, local, or restrictions per the home owner association (HOA). I cannot stress enough that as a landlord, you should take time to become familiar with your local and state laws as well as any applicable HOA covenants and restrictions.

KEYS TO HIRING A PROPERTY MANAGEMENT

CHAPTER XII

KEYS TO HIRING A PROPERTY MANAGEMENT PROFESSIONAL

After reading this book, the goal is that you have the foundational elements to manage your property and be extraordinarily successful. However, if after reading this book or after deciding to explore the process, you change your mind, it is okay! There are many reasons why an individual would decide to hire a professional property manager and it boils down to preference.

Below is a list of what I have determined are the more common reasons for hiring a professional. Additionally, what you should look for in a property manager if you make that decision down the landlord road.

Time Value

Being a landlord sounds great until you get the late-night call about a busted pipe, clogged toilet or even a blown bulb. Worst of all, the call while on vacation regarding the HVAC that totally disrupts your sunbathing or martinis by the pool. These scenarios, along with the fact that as a novice landlord it is likely you will still have a "day job" while building your portfolio, add up to not enough hours in the day.

Thusly, the number one reason to hire a professional management company is time. Most landlords do not have the time, daily, to personally, manage their properties. By hiring a manager, you are giving yourself additional time to do the things you love and enjoy outside of your rental property.

Negotiating Skills

Do you ever try to negotiate with yourself? Well, the same dilemma can become a factor when dealing with residents. As the owner you have a goal to meet your best interests, sometimes contrary to best business practices. It can be a bit cumbersome when trying to negotiate with tenants, vendors, contractors, insurance agents, and HOA representatives, when you are fully aware of your own needs, processes, procedures, and desires for your investment and your non-refundable tickets to Maui.

Hiring a professional with strong negotiating skills is an irreplaceable benefit to owners. It is their job to make sure your property is maintained daily. In doing so, we may need to negotiate on your behalf with contractors, vendors, homeowners 'associations, banks, and even directly with the tenant. Negotiating skills are extremely important because it allows you to get the best deals on contract work and eliminates the need for communication between you and the tenant. This communication can carry over to addressing HOA concerns, city violations, and even legal matters.

Legal Knowledge

Another great reason to use a property manager is for their knowledge of tenant and landlord laws. Each state has specific guidelines in place that dictate what a landlord can and cannot do with respect to tenants. A professional property manager will know the laws. Being the professional means, it is their job to ensure those laws and regulations are followed to the fullest and to remain abreast of challenges to the laws that may impact your investment and residents.

Rental Rates

Hiring a property manager allows you to set and maintain the best rental rates. Property managers understand the market, the location, and the demographics of the tenants who will be renting your home. They constantly study the market to be able to advise you on what will be the best rent, to ensure the best chances to keep your property occupied.

What are the costs of hiring a PM?

One of the most important questions you should ask a potential Property Manager is regarding their fee structure. There is an array of fees a PM may charge, however here a few to reference: an administrative fee or set-up fee, a monthly property management fee, and a tenant marketing fee. There could be other fees, so this list is not meant to be all-inclusive. Remember that each PM/PM Firm has its own guidelines and experiences that determine its pricing strategy. The fees listed below are simply essentials to know and a good place to begin comparison shopping for and hiring a property manager.

Set-Up Fee

The set-up fee is paid upon contract, and it may cover your initial marketing, the initial move-in inspection and getting you set-up in all the office's software. This fee also covers getting your future tenant set-up in a database or property management system. This fee may also include initial marketing and validating data you provide of the home such as square footage.

Management Fee

The monthly management fee can be a flat fee or percentage based. Every company varies thus it is important to do your research and ensure you fully understand the fee structure of your elected property manager.

Marketing Fee

A marketing fee may be charged per tenant. It is imperative as the landlord you know this and that their caveats to each PM's assessment of this fee.

These are very basic fees however the list can go on. Your property management agreement should spell out any fee that will be assessed. Always review your agreement before signing. If there is any area where you are unsure, ask the Property Manager you are interviewing to explain and preferably show you, in writing, what she/he has stated.

Essential Property Management Attributes

Here is a list of the top attributes every property manager should have:

1. Trustworthiness

Your investment properties may be your largest asset outside of your personal residence and a major part of your overall wealth strategy. Ask yourself if you would trust that person with your retirement. Your children's education. You cannot afford to overlook or glaze over the element of trust in any business strategy. Real estate is no different.

2. Experience

Experience with your type of property is paramount. You want to hire a professional who has experience with the type of property you acquired. Whether you invest in commercial, residential, multi-family there are going to be elements that are specific to each which require specialized expertise. Commercial properties and tenants have different nuances than residential. Think about it in another realm. Would you hire a tax attorney to handle your divorce, with the same level of confidence as a divorce attorney? An individual with experience will be able to identify opportunities to add, better, and maximize your investment, by recognizing value-add opportunities and help increase your NOI due to their knowledge of rent and expense benchmarks for this type of property.

3. Financial and Accounting Acumen

It is now common, in many commercial real estate companies, to separate accounting and property management responsibilities. Unfortunately, this means there is a large pool of professionals with little to no understanding of financial statements and accounting. Investors should carefully interview potential companies and, if needed, engage the assistance of their CPA in selecting a firm.

4. Their Tenant Screening Process

The best property managers are ones who screen tenants by conducting background, credit, and reference checks. There was a reason I stressed this for you. A professional PM is no different. It is vital to find property managers who are professional, reputable, and well-established to keep both the landlords and tenants satisfied with the arrangement, for the long term.

5. Their Turnover Rates and Cost of Vacancy

Investors often focus too much on the PM fee. That is a valid part of your weeding process but should not be the sole focus. A primary focus, while choosing a PM, should be their turnover process. If your rent is $1,000 and PM is 10%, you pay $100 per month. At 9%, you only save $10 per month. Consider the cost of vacancy. The same unit costs $30 in lost income per day when vacant. Immerse yourself in the process. Schedule a viewing of the property and see what their process looks like. In so doing, you will see what your potential renters experience. Are you impressed? If not, that's something to consider.

6. Their Technology

Even pre-pandemic, more and more PMs are using technology, to varying levels. However, you not only want to look for use of technology but a company or individual that offers a full package of services integrated with technology. You want a property manager who knows how to leverage the data about your property to make precise and proactive recommendations. Additionally, analyze whether they are integrating on-site services. Those PMs are better able to leverage that technology and execute it to maintain and protect your investment.

7. Local Knowledge

Be careful to not get hypnotized by "I have 1000 customers." Logic says that level of business means they are the best. The question then becomes "How effectively are they at handling each of those 100/500/1000 properties?". Despite advances in technology and premium integrated technology suites, only so much can be done in the office. It is vital that the Property Manager you choose has a "boots on the ground" strategy integrated into their services and can check on the property in person. Information coming in through a computer program cannot replace someone that can and will regularly drive or stop by. It is that part of their management strategy that could catch any issues with the building or community before they become problems.

8. Ability to Communicate

There are some things that cannot be taught. You either have it or you don't. Learned competencies are essential but for a property management professional, you need a communicator. Communication or people skills is one of the first things I, personally, look for in absolutely everyone representing and of my business interests.

9. Financial Transparency

This should be #1! A rate schedule on managing a property is not the only financial consideration when hiring a property manager. It is just as important to know the company's policies for other charges including maintenance, leasing, and other activities. Additional financial considerations are: Do they send you the bill directly or do they markup maintenance or other orders? Do they take a fee or percentage for leasing units? Their transparency, forced or uncovered through your due diligence, will alleviate common misunderstandings later.

10. Availability and Responsiveness

Believe it or not, investment real estate can be a 24/7 commitment. Therefore, hire a Property Manager. Remember, though, that simply hiring a PM does not alleviate your responsibilities to your investment, unless they have systems in place to answer and handle issues that arise 24/7. You will need a PM that dedicates their time or designates someone with the time to ensure your tenants are happy and your property is being cared for. Long-term occupancy depends on it.

11. Values Cost-Effectiveness

There are things involved in managing investment real estate that HAVE TO be handled so much differently than your personal property. There are uncontrollable costs like insurance, mortgage payment, and taxes. They are what they are and changing them generally means a dramatic change to your investment.

There are also controllable costs like turn times, marketing and maintenance, or property upkeep. So instead of choosing to change things like how often you mow the lawn—which can cause issues from the tenant satisfaction standpoint—it is better to find a more cost-effective strategy. Perhaps, finding another vendor. Sometimes it is not about eliminating a cost but controlling it. PMs who get that make the best choices that keep the bottom-line foremost in their management strategy while always keeping tenant happiness in mind, as well.

12. A Long-Term Mindset

Real estate is like a marriage. When you make that decision to forge ahead, you do so for the long haul. So, make sure to surround yourself with individuals, agents, property managers, and accountants—your team—that all have that marriage-minded way of thinking. It is in all parties' best interests to remember your goals as the investor and the roles they each play to achieve those goals, to the benefit of each member of the team.

MANAGEMENT IN A CRISIS: WHAT COVID-19 TAUGHT ME ABOUT PROPERTY MANAGEMENT

I call this chapter a "bonus chapter," because, at the outset of the writing and virtual completion of this project, the novel coronavirus was not a thing. At least not to the level that one would need processes and procedures in place to handle it. Yet...here we are, and it is only fitting that as I've worked so hard to stress to you due diligence, in all things throughout this book, I do mine.

Whether it is the H1N1 flu, whooping cough, or COVID-19, there are just some things that even the most experienced landlord cannot predict. Notice I did not say "cannot plan for". Crises, though unpredictable, can be managed with proper planning, procedures, and policies that give you the flexibility to assess, adapt accordingly, and evaluate—on a deeper level—how prepared you are to work with your tenant, keep your tenant and ultimately protect your investment.

With other crises, those mentioned specifically, there was not the widespread issue of furloughs and businesses closing affecting the employment status of so many across the country. COVID-19 has posed issues and tested processes in a myriad of unprecedented ways. However, though it was unpredictable and presented unprecedented obstacles, the foundational problem to be solved was the same as any other for an investment property owner or property manager. How do I maintain and protect the success of this investment?

First things first. You must consider those not or not yet impacted financially by the pandemic. For example, essential workers. Some have been spared from job loss and accompanying loss of revenue, by virtue of the industry or capacity in which they work. However, rent still needs to be collected (socially distanced in person, mail, etc.) and routine inspections conducted. Any of the number of issues I have previously had occasion to mention could happen, also. Pandemic or not, appliances continue to need maintenance and HVAC needs to be prepared for winter. Life, unfortunately or fortunately, goes on.

So, how do you assure the tenant that whoever needs to enter their home has their health and safety in mind while finding reliable, reputable tradespeople? And then, what measures can, or should you take to make sure they have already adapted their services to include proper sanitation practices? In addition to that, how do you convey to your tenant the need for them to do their due diligence, for the health and hygiene of any staff or repairmen that may need to access their home?

I know it's hard to wrap your head around. Remember, I have encountered the dirty diapers and cement poured in pipes. Pandemic...unprecedented. What isn't unprecedented, is the absolute necessity to move past the feeling of "what now?" to "here is what we are going to do, now, and how we'll adapt for the next...crisis".

On March 13, 2020, while traveling to DC, I received word that the country was slowly beginning to have immediate shutdowns in different areas. By Monday, March 16, 2020, I had returned to Charlotte, NC to find that our city, my home base of business operations, had also shut down for the safety of the community. Our office had to begin immediately communicating with owners and tenants advising on how our office would operate in what would be a year-long (at least) experience of virtual operations amid a pandemic. In this "new normal," I had to learn to think outside of the box to keep residents updated on resources to not just pay rent but to remain healthy, sane, and safe! Reflecting on building relationships with tenants as a landlord, this year was vital in putting that concept into practice.

Millions of tenants are facing the loss of income or have on some level or another during this time. In some cases, it may not even be a tenant but someone the tenant has now become financially responsible for, causing financial stress that may lead to issues of timely, consistent rent payments.

Even with lease language in place to deal with late rents and built-in grace periods, COVID-19 has presented some with the need for grace periods but for an unknown amount of time. It is not just someone unexpectedly losing their job. It's potentially tens of thousands in one geographic area, waiting for phases to progress and communities reopen and businesses to rebound, and rehire. So, how do you handle an investment that was possibly paying for itself, that you must now carry, should you find yourself able and/or wanting to keep that good tenant, until the world gets back to normal.

One of the strategies I use when onboarding property management clients and coaching landlords is being financially prepared to cover the costs of their investments for 3-6 months when or if a tenant does not pay. This implementation saved many of my portfolio clients from financial stress during COVID-19. If you don't take anything away from this book, please note that the fiscal responsibility for your investment will always reside in your hands. Be prepared for when the tenant does not pay and if there is no tenant because there will a time when this occurs. Prayerfully, never like what has been experienced in 2020-2021.

Making it through a pandemic in respect to property preservation, was the result of strong partnerships, having reliable, professional, prudent service partners that were able to adjust and adapt to the current COVID-19 environment, allowed resident maintenance requests to continue being safely answered and resolved. Your investment property is a business and who you trust to handle repairs and routine maintenance matters. In a crisis is the last moment in which you want to regret your choice of vendor partners.

No one could have predicted the effects of 18 months of a pandemic on landlords however prudent early financial planning and foresight has truly saved many from financial ruin. Plan for the unknown by acknowledging the unknown can and will happen!

CONCLUSION

Buying and holding property is not for the faint of heart and being a landlord has its fair share of ups and downs. Property Management with a P.O.P.P.®, I hope has given insight to the novice landlord on how to evaluate and create profit, build processes and procedures to secure long-term occupancy and gain principles to preserve their property.

When you opened this book, you had a desire to learn and create a pathway to creating wealth through real estate. May this book be used to begin and execute your plan!

ABOUT THE AUTHOR

Sherkica Miller-McIntyre dived headfirst into real estate investing 18 years ago providing lease buy-back options to new home construction buyers whose deals were falling through. Buying directly from the builder allowed her to capitalize on both the leasing and sales market in the early 2000s. Building passive income from the leases and earning five-figure profits on 12-24 months transactions lead Sherkica to desire to earn an additional source of income... the commission!

After earning her sales license in December 2004, Sherkica immediately gained her Broker's license in 2005 and ultimately earned the title of Broker In Change and Property Manager of Carod Properties. Sherkica, along with her supportive husband and business partner, Gary, has been able to exponentially grow Carod Properties, one of the top property management firms in the Charlotte market.

Having served over 500 investor clients and more than 1500 resident families in North and South Carolina, matching the needs of investors across the world to the housing needs of residents, Sherkica has gained the title of "One Stop Shop for Investors".

Sherkica holds both a BSBA and MBA with an emphasis in Marketing. She has over 25 years of experience in Customer Service and Management, 15 years of experience in Financial Services which include Consulting and Mortgage Lending. She is currently an active member of NARPM® (National Association of Residential Property Managers) where she has served as President, Vice-President, and Charity and Members Services Chairperson for the Charlotte, NC Chapter. She sits on several national committees for the organization to include Professional Development, National Member Services, and the Annual Convention and Trade Show Committee. Because of her dedication and service to the organization she has been featured in the National NARPM publication, currently holds the RPM® designation and is currently working towards her MPM®, Master Property Management designation.

Sherkica and her husband are the very proud parents of four amazing children. She is also a "GlamMa" of both an adorable Alaskan Husky and Pomsky, loves to travel, and has found a passion for adult coloring books. Her only issue right now is finding the time to pursue her new passion for coloring.

To book Sherkica Miller-McIntyre to present a workshop, as a consultant, or training visit www.pmwithapopp.com

ACKNOWLEDGMENTS

When sitting down to write my acknowledgments, I struggled. I know I would need another book to include everyone's name who either directly or indirectly played a key role in helping me arrive where I am.

I also know, that because of the gratefulness in my heart and my deeds, they prayerfully all know of their importance to me. That said, there are a few people that were key in my professional development that I would like to take the time to acknowledge.

The Carias/Rodriguez family. You trusted me to be your broker. This show of faith led to an ultimate show of family...allowing my family to purchase your firm. I work extremely hard, daily, to gain the trust of others & to continue shining the light you saw in me.

Deidre Johnson. My colleague that inspires me to keep paying it forward. Thank you for showing me that a big part of my legacy is not in what I have attained but what I have given back to help others. Thank you also for always taking my calls, I know your ears hurt.

Amy Phillips-Davis. My heart is heavy as I thank and acknowledge the woman that was there at the onset of this great adventure. Thank you, Amy, for being there at the beginning, before I even knew where I was trying to go. You were and will forever be an inspiration. I shall never forget the role you played in me becoming, Sherkica Miller-McIntyre, Investor/Broker/Property Manager and Coach/Mentor to others just as you were to me. I only regret that I end this project with thanks and a sincere prayer that you are proud, as you Rest In Heaven!